Everyday A Phrasebook for Dubai Travelers

Essential Arabic Expressions for Your Seamless Dubai Journey

Aziz Barakat

Table of Content

Everyday Arabic Phrasebook for Dubai Travelers... 1

Copyright © 2

Table of Content 3

Introduction 5

Pronunciation Guide for Learning Arabic 11

Greetings and Polite Expressions......................... 17

Getting Around and Transportation 25

Asking for Directions... 30

Taking a Taxi.. 38

Using Public Transport.. 43

Renting a Car... 51

Airport Vocabulary.. 56

Arrivals and Departures 60

Dining and Food 64

Dining Out Phrases.. 73

Shopping for Groceries 77

Introduction

Welcome to the "Everyday Arabic Phrasebook for Dubai Travelers"!

Whether you're visiting Dubai for business or pleasure, you're about to embark on an exciting journey to one of the most vibrant and culturally diverse cities in the world.

Dubai is a city of contrasts, where ancient traditions meet modern innovations, and where people from all corners of the globe come together to create a unique and dynamic atmosphere.

In this phrasebook, we've compiled a comprehensive collection of essential Arabic phrases and expressions that will help you navigate Dubai with confidence.

While English is widely spoken in Dubai, learning a few key Arabic phrases can go a long way in enhancing your travel experience.

It demonstrates respect for the local culture and can also make your interactions with locals more meaningful.

Why Learn Arabic for Your Dubai Trip?

Dubai is a melting pot of cultures, with residents hailing from over 200 nationalities.

While many Dubaians are fluent in English, Arabic remains the official language of the United Arab Emirates.

Learning a bit of Arabic can open doors to deeper cultural understanding and make your stay more enjoyable. It can help you negotiate in local markets, order delicious dishes at traditional restaurants, and engage in friendly conversations with locals who will appreciate your efforts to speak their language.

What You'll Find in This Phrasebook

This phrasebook is designed to be a practical and user-friendly resource for travelers of all levels of language proficiency.

Whether you're a complete beginner or have some prior knowledge of Arabic, you'll find useful phrases, key vocabulary, and cultural insights to help you connect with the people of Dubai and make the most of your stay.

In the following chapters, you'll discover phrases for everyday situations, such as greeting locals, ordering food, getting around the city, and exploring Dubai's rich cultural heritage.

We've also included tips on pronunciation to help you speak with confidence.

How to Use This Phrasebook

Feel free to use this phrasebook in the way that best suits your needs. You can read it cover to cover or jump directly to the section that's most relevant to your current situation.

Each chapter is organized logically, making it easy to find the phrases you need quickly.

Before we dive into the phrases and vocabulary, take a moment to review the pronunciation guide, which will assist you in pronouncing Arabic words correctly.

Don't be discouraged by the Arabic script; we've included transliterations to help you with pronunciation, and you'll find that many locals are more than willing to help you learn and practice.

So, whether you're preparing for your first visit to Dubai or looking to enhance your travel experience, this phrasebook is your trusted companion.

Embrace the diversity, warmth, and hospitality of Dubai by speaking a bit of Arabic, and you'll find that your journey becomes not just a trip, but a true adventure filled with meaningful connections and unforgettable moments.

Safe travels, and enjoy your time in Dubai!

Pronunciation Guide for Learning Arabic

Learning the pronunciation of Arabic can be challenging for beginners, but with practice and a basic understanding of the Arabic alphabet, you can make significant progress.

Here's a simplified pronunciation guide to help you get started:

Consonants:

ب **(bāʾ)** - Pronounced like the English "b" in "bat."

ت **(tāʾ)** - Similar to the English "t" in "top."

ث **(thāʾ)** - Similar to the English "th" in "think," but with more emphasis on the "th" sound.

ج **(jīm)** - Pronounced like the English "j" in "jump."

ح **(ḥāʾ)** - This sound is pronounced from the back of your throat, somewhat like clearing your throat.

خ **(khāʾ)** - A guttural sound, similar to the Scottish "loch" or the German "Bach."

د **(dāl)** - Similar to the English "d" in "dog."

ذ **(dhāl)** - Similar to the English "th" in "this," but with more emphasis on the "th" sound.

ر **(rāʾ)** - Similar to the English "r" sound but slightly rolled or tapped.

ز **(zāy)** - Similar to the English "z" in "zebra."

س **(sīn)** - Similar to the English "s" in "sand."

ش **(shīn)** - Similar to the English "sh" in "shoe."

ص **(ṣād)** - A deep "s" sound, similar to "ss" in "hiss," but more pronounced.

ض **(ḍād)** - Similar to "d" but with a heavier and deeper sound.

ط **(ṭāʾ)** - A deep "t" sound, pronounced with the tongue against the upper front teeth.

ظ **(ẓāʾ)** - Similar to "z" but with a heavier and deeper sound.

ع **(ʿayn)** - A guttural sound unique to Arabic. Try making a "gh" sound from the back of your throat.

غ **(ghayn)** - Another guttural sound, similar to the French "r" in "Paris" or the Dutch "g."

ف **(fāʾ)** - Similar to the English "f" in "food."

ق **(qāf)** - Pronounced as a deep "k" sound made further back in the throat.

ك **(kāf)** - Similar to the English "k" in "kite."

ل **(lām)** - Similar to the English "l" in "love."

م **(mīm)** - Similar to the English "m" in "mother."

ن **(nūn)** - Similar to the English "n" in "now."

ه **(hāʾ)** - Similar to the English "h" in "house."

و **(wāw)** - Similar to the English "w" in "water."

ي **(yāʾ)** - Similar to the English "y" in "yes."

Vowels:

Arabic has both short and long vowels. Short vowels are not usually written in the script but are crucial for pronunciation. Here are the basic vowels:

ا **(alif)** - Similar to the English "a" in "cat."

و **(wāw)** - Similar to the English "o" in "go."

ي **(yā')** - Similar to the English "ee" in "see."

Important Pronunciation Tips:

Arabic is a consonant-heavy language, and the pronunciation of consonants can change slightly depending on their position within a word.

Pay attention to the vowels, as changing the vowel can change the meaning of a word.

Practice listening to native speakers to improve your pronunciation.

Remember that pronunciation can vary slightly across different Arabic dialects, so the above guide focuses on Modern Standard Arabic, which serves as a common form for communication across the Arab world.

Greetings and Polite Expressions

Below are some common greetings and polite expressions in Arabic, along with their English translations and approximate sound intonations.

Please note that Arabic pronunciation can vary slightly depending on the region, but these general pronunciations should help you get started.

1. مرحبًا (Marhaban) - Hello

English Translation: Hello

Sound Intonation: ma-ra-HA-ban

2. صباح الخير **(Sabaḥ al-khayr)** - Good morning

English Translation: Good morning

Sound Intonation: sa-BAH al-KHA-yer

3. الخ ير مساء (Masa' al-khayr) - Good evening- The same word for Good Afternoon.

English Translation: Good afternoon/Good evening

Sound Intonation: ma-SA-a al-KHA-yer

4. ك يف حالك؟ (Kayfa ḥāluk?) - How are you?

English Translation: How are you?

Sound Intonation: KAY-fa HA-luk?

5. أنا ب خ ير، شكرًا **(Ana bikhayr, shukran)** - I'm fine, thank you

English Translation: I'm fine, thank you

Sound Intonation: A-na bi-KHA-yer, SHUK-ran

6. ا سمك؟ ما (Mā ismak?) - What's your name?

English Translation: What's your name?

Sound Intonation: MAH is-MAK?

7. ا سمي **[Your Name] (Ismi [Your Name])** - My name is [Your Name]

English Translation: My name is [Your Name]

Sound Intonation: IS-mi [Your Name]

8. ت شرف ت لقائك ب (Tasharraftu biliqā'ik) - Nice to meet you

English Translation: Nice to meet you

Sound Intonation: ta-shar-RAT-tu bi-li-QA-i-k

9. من فضلك (**Min faḍlik**) - Please

English Translation: Please

Sound Intonation: min fa-DLIK

10. شكرًا (Shukran) - Thank you

- English Translation: Thank you

- Sound Intonation: SHOOK-ran

11. على الرحب والسعة (ʿalā al-rahb wal-saʿah) - You're welcome

- English Translation: You're welcome

- Sound Intonation: ʿa-LA al-RAHB wal-sa-AH

12. عذرًا ('adhraan) - Excuse me / Sorry

- English Translation: Excuse me / Sorry

- Sound Intonation: ʿad-DHRAAN

13. ن عم (Na'am) - Yes

- English Translation: Yes

- Sound Intonation: NA-am

14. لا (Lā) - No

- English Translation: No

- Sound Intonation: LAA

15. وداعًا (Wadā'an) - Goodbye

- English Translation: Goodbye

- Sound Intonation: wa-DA-aan

16. ال لقاء إ لى (Ila al-liqāʾ) - See you later

- English Translation: See you later

- Sound Intonation: IL-lah al-LEE-QAA

17. سعيدًا يومًا لك أتّ مـ نى (Atamannā lak yawman sa'īdan) - Have a nice day

- English Translation: Have a nice day

- Sound Intonation: At-ta-man-NA lak yaw-man sa-EE-dan

18. أنا آسف ع لى قدانك فـ (Ana ʾāsif ʿalā faqdānik) - I'm sorry for your loss

- English Translation: I'm sorry for your loss

- Sound Intonation: A-na A-sif ʿa-LA faq-DA-nik

19. الله   بارك ي يك ف (Allah yibārik fīk) - May God bless you

- English Translation: May God bless you

- Sound Intonation: Al-lah yi-baa-RIK FEEK

20. Where are you from?

Arabic: من أي ن أن ت؟ (Min ayna anta/anti?)

English Translation: Where are you from?

Sound Intonation: meen AY-na AN-ta/AN-tee?

21. Do you speak English?

Arabic: هل تحدث ت الإن جل يزية؟ (Hal tatahaddath al-ingliziyya?)

English Translation: Do you speak English?

Sound Intonation: hal ta-ta-had-DATH al-in-glee-ZEE-ya?

These phrases will help you ask about someone's origin and language skills in Arabic. Practice the sound intonations to ensure clear communication.

These expressions, along with their sound intonations, will help you communicate with confidence and politeness when speaking Arabic.

Remember to practice the pronunciation to improve your conversational skills.

Getting Around and Transportation

Here are some common words and phrases related to getting around and transportation in Arabic, along with their English translations and sound intonations:

1. Transportation - ال نقل و سائ ل (Wasā'il al-naql)

Sound Intonation: wa-saa-il al-NA-qil

2. Car - س يارة (Sayyārah)

Sound Intonation: say-YAA-rah

3. Bus - حاف لة (Ḥāfilah)

Sound Intonation: HA-fi-lah

4. Taxi - سيارة أجرة (Sayyārah ajrah)

Sound Intonation: say-YAA-rah aj-RAH

5. Train - قطار (Qiṭār)

Sound Intonation: qi-TAAR

6. Metro/Subway - مترو (Mitrū)

Sound Intonation: mee-TRO

7. Airport - مطار (Maṭār)

Sound Intonation: ma-TAAR

8. Station - محطة (Maḥṭah)

Sound Intonation: maḥ-TAH

9. Ticket - تذكرة (Tadhkirah)

Sound Intonation: tad-KHEE-rah

10. Schedule - زم ني جدول (Jadwal zamnī)

- Sound Intonation: jad-WAL zam-NEE

11. Platform - م نصة (Manshah)

- Sound Intonation: man-SHAH

12. Departure - مغادرة (Mughādarah)

- **Sound Intonation: mu-ghaa-DAR-ah**

13. Arrival - و صول (Wuṣūl)

- Sound Intonation: wa-SOOL

14. Ticket Counter - ال تذاكر ش باك (Shibāk at-tadhakir)

- Sound Intonation: shi-BAK at-tad-ha-KIR

15. Map - خريطة (Kharīṭah)

- **Sound Intonation: khah-REE-tah**

16. Direction - اتجاه (Itijāh)

- Sound Intonation: i-ti-JAAH

17. Stop - توقف (Tawaqquf)

- Sound Intonation: ta-wak-KUF

18. Ticket Machine - جهاز بيع التذاكر (Jihāz bayʿ at-tadhakir)

- Sound Intonation: ji-HAAZ beeʿ at-tad-ha-KIR

19. Driver - سائق (Sā'iḳ)

- Sound Intonation: saa-IK

20. Pedestrian - مشاة (Mushāh)

- Sound Intonation: mu-SHAH

These words and phrases will be helpful when navigating transportation and getting around in Arabic-speaking regions.

Practice the sound intonations to ensure clear communication while traveling.

Asking for Directions

Here are some common words and phrases related to asking for directions in Arabic, along with their English translations and sound intonations:

1. Directions - اتجاهات (Itijāhāt)

Sound Intonation: i-ti-JAA-haat

2. Where is...? - أين...؟ (Ayna...?)

Sound Intonation: AY-na...?

3. How do I get to...? - كيف يمكنني الوصول إلى...؟ (Kayfa yumkinuni al-wusul ila...?)

Sound Intonation: KAY-fa yoom-ki-NU-nee al-woo-SOOL ila...?

4. Street - شارع (Sharī')

Sound Intonation: sha-REH

5. Road - طريق (Ṭarīq)

Sound Intonation: ṭa-REEQ

6. Turn left - انعطف يسارًا (Inʿaṭaf yasāran)

Sound Intonation: in-a-TAF ya-SA-ran

7. Turn right - انعطف يمينًا (Inʿaṭaf yamīnan)

Sound Intonation: in-a-TAF ya-MEE-nan

8. Go straight - اذهب مباشرةً (Idẖab mubāširatan)

Sound Intonation: idh-HAB mu-BA-shee-ra-tan

9. Stop here - وقف تنا ه (Tawaqquf huna)

Sound Intonation: ta-wak-KUF hoo-NA

10. Intersection - قاطع ت (Taqaṭu')

- Sound Intonation: ta-qa-TU

11. Bridge - جسر (Jisr)

- Sound Intonation: jisr

12. Traffic light - مرور إشارة (Ishārah murūr)

- Sound Intonation: i-SHA-rah mu-ROOR

13. Roundabout - دوار (Dawwar)

- Sound Intonation: DOW-war

14. Landmark - معروفة علامة ('ālamah ma'rūfah)

- Sound Intonation: 'a-LA-mah ma-ROO-fah

15. Near - قريب (Qarīb)

- Sound Intonation: qa-REEB

16. Far - بعيد (Ba'īd)

- Sound Intonation: ba-EED

17. Map - خريطة (Kharițah)

- Sound Intonation: kha-REE-tah

18. GPS - الملاحة نظام (Naẓām al-malāḥah)

- Sound Intonation: na-ZAAM al-ma-la-HA

19. North - الشمال (Ash-Shamāl)

- Sound Intonation: ash-sha-MAAL

20. South - الجنوب (Al-Janūb)

- Sound Intonation: al-ja-NOOB

21. East - الشرق (Ash-Sharq)

- Sound Intonation: ash-SHARQ

22. West - الغرب (Al-Gharb)

- Sound Intonation: al-GHARB

23. Straight ahead - مباشرة أمامك (Mubāshiratan amāmak)

- Sound Intonation: mu-BA-shee-ra-tan a-MA-mak

24. Distance - المسافة (Al-masāfah)

- Sound Intonation: al-ma-SA-fah

25. How far is it? - كم هي بعيدة؟ (Kam hiya baʿīdah?)

- Sound Intonation: kam HEE-ya ba-EEdah?

26. Can you show me on the map? - هل يمكنك أن تريني على الخريطة؟ (Hal yumkinuka an turīnī ʿalā al-kharīṭah?)

- Sound Intonation: hal yoom-ki-NOO-ka an tu-REE-nee ʿa-LA al-kha-REE-tah?

27. I'm lost - لقد ضللت (Laqad ḍallalt)

- Sound Intonation: la-QAD ḍal-LALT

28. Can you help me? - هل يمكنك مساعدتي ؟ (Hal yumkinuka musāʿadatī?)

- Sound Intonation: hal yoom-ki-NOO-ka mu-saa-ʿa-DA-tee?

29. Where is the nearest...? - أي ن أق رب...؟ (Ayna aqrab...?)

- Sound Intonation: AY-na a-KRAB...?

30. Is it on this street? - هل هو في هذا ال شارع ؟ (Hal huwa fī hadā ash-shāri'?)

- Sound Intonation: hal HOO-wa fee ha-ZA ash-sha-REE-'?

31. Can you write it down for me? - هل يـمـكـنك تـهـا كـتابـ ؟ لي (Hal yumkinuka kitābatahā lī?)

- Sound Intonation: hal yoom-ki-NOO-ka kee-TA-ba-ha LEE?

32. Excuse me, can you give me directions? - عذرًا، هل يـمـكـنك أن تـعـطـيـني الاتـجاهات؟ ('adhraan, hal yumkinuka an ta'ṭīnī al-itujaahāt?)

- Sound Intonation: ʿadh-RAAN, hal yoom-ki-NOO-ka an ta-ʿa-TEE-nee al-i-tu-JAA-haat?

33. Landmark - علامة (ʿālamah)

- Sound Intonation: ʿa-LA-mah

34. Road sign - لافتة (Lāfṭah)

- Sound Intonation: laaf-TAH

35. Path - مسار (Masār)

- Sound Intonation: ma-SAAR

These words and phrases will be helpful when asking for directions in Arabic-speaking regions. Practice the sound intonations to ensure clear communication while navigating unfamiliar places.

Taking a Taxi

Here are some common words and phrases related to taking a taxi in Arabic, along with their English translations and sound intonations:

1. Taxi - سيارة أجرة (Sayyārah ajrah)

Sound Intonation: say-YAA-rah aj-RAH

2. Taxi stand - محطة سيارات الأجرة (Maḥṭah sayyārāt al-ajrah)

Sound Intonation: maḥ-TAH say-yaa-RAAT al-aj-RAH

3. Taxi driver - سائق سيارة الأجرة (Sā'iḳ sayyārah al-ajrah)

Sound Intonation: saa-IK say-YAA-rah al-aj-RAH

4. Take me to... - خذني إلى... (Khudhnī ilā...)

Sound Intonation: khudh-NEE ila...

5. How much is the fare? - كم التكلفة؟ (Kam at-taklifah?)

Sound Intonation: kam at-tak-LI-fah?

6. Meter - عداد (ʿadad)

Sound Intonation: ʿa-DAD

7. Speed up - أسرع (Asraʿ)

Sound Intonation: as-RA

8. Slow down - بطء (Biṭʾ)

Sound Intonation: bi-TS

9. Stop here - توقف هنا (Tawaqquf huna)

Sound Intonation: ta-wak-KUF hoo-NA

10. Left - ي سار (Yasār)

- Sound Intonation: ya-SAAR

11. Right - ي م ين (Yamīn)

- Sound Intonation: ya-MEEN

12. U-turn - دورة (Dawrah)

- Sound Intonation: DOW-rah

13. Traffic - ال مرور حـ ركة (Ḥarakat al-murūr)

- Sound Intonation: ḥa-RAK-at al-mu-ROOR

14. Seatbelt - الأم ان حزام (Ḥizām al-amān)

- Sound Intonation: ḥi-ZAAM al-a-MAAN

15. Keep the change - خلّ الباقي (Khallil baqī)

- Sound Intonation: kha-LEEL ba-QEE

16. Address - عنوان (ʿunwān)

- Sound Intonation: ʿu-NWAAN

17. Receipt - إيصال (Iṣāl)

- Sound Intonation: i-SAA-al

18. I need a taxi - أحتاج سيارة أجرة (Uḥtāj sayyārah ajrah)

- Sound Intonation: uḥ-TAAJ say-YAA-rah aj-RAH

19. Can you wait for me? - هل يمكنك الانتظار لي؟ (Hal yumkinuka al-intiẓār lī?)

- Sound Intonation: hal yoom-ki-NOO-ka al-in-TIZAAR LEE?

20. Take me to the airport - الـمطار إ لى خذني

(Khudhnī ilā al-maṭār)

- Sound Intonation: khudh-NEE ila al-ma-TAAR

These words and phrases will be useful when taking a taxi and communicating with taxi drivers in Arabic-speaking regions.

Practice the sound intonations to ensure smooth interactions.

Using Public Transport

Here are some common words and phrases related to using public transport in Arabic, along with their English translations and sound intonations:

1. Public Transport - ال عامة ال نقل و سائ ل (Wasā'il an-naql al-ʿāmah)

Sound Intonation: wa-saa-il an-NAQL al-ʿAA-mah

2. Bus - حاف لة (Ḥāfilah)

Sound Intonation: HA-fi-lah

3. Bus Stop - ال حاف لات محطة (Maḥṭah al-ḥāfilāt)

Sound Intonation: maḥ-TAH al-ha-FEE-lat

4. Train - ق طار (Qiṭār)

Sound Intonation: qi-TAAR

5. Train Station - محطة ال قطار (Maḥṭah al-qiṭār)

Sound Intonation: maḥ-TAH al-qi-TAAR

6. Metro/Subway - م ترو (Mitrū)

Sound Intonation: mee-TRO

7. Tram - ت رام (Trām)

Sound Intonation: TRAAM

8. Ticket - تذ ذكر (Tadhkirah)

Sound Intonation: tad-KHEE-rah

9. Ticket Machine - جهاز بيع ال تذاكر (Jihāz bay' at-tadhakir)

Sound Intonation: ji-HAAZ beeʿ at-tad-ha-KIR

10. Timetable - زم ني جدول (Jadwal zamnī)

- Sound Intonation: jad-WAL zam-NEE

11. Fare - ت كل فة (Taklifah)

- Sound Intonation: tak-LI-fah

12. Platform - م ن صة (Manshah)

- Sound Intonation: man-SHAH

13. Boarding Pass - ال صعود ب طاقة (Biṭāqah al-ṣuʿūd)

- Sound Intonation: bi-TAA-qah al-ṣu-OO-d

14. Seat - م قعد (Maqʿad)

- Sound Intonation: maq-AAD

15. Line/Route - خط (Khaṭṭ)

- Sound Intonation: khaṭṭ

16. Platform - منصة (Manshah)

- Sound Intonation: man-SHAH

17. Stop - توقف (Tawaqquf)

- Sound Intonation: ta-wak-KUF

18. Stand clear of the doors - ابتعد عن الأبواب (Ibtaʿid ʿan al-abwāb)

- Sound Intonation: ib-ta-ʿid ʿan al-a-BO-aab

19. Transfer - انتقال (Intiqāl)

- Sound Intonation: in-TI-qal

20. Board the train/bus - اصعد إلى القطار/الحافلة (Iṣʿad ilā al-qiṭār/al-ḥāfilah)

- Sound Intonation: is-ʿad ila al-qi-TAAR/al-HA-fi-lah

21. Metro Line - الم ترو خط (Khaṭṭ al-mitrū)

- Sound Intonation: khaṭṭ al-mee-TRO

22. Bus Route - الحاف لة مسار (Masār al-ḥāfilah)

- Sound Intonation: ma-SAAR al-HA-fi-lah

23. Train Schedule - القطار مواع يد جدول (Jadwal mawāʿīd al-qiṭār)

- Sound Intonation: jad-WAL ma-WAA-eed al-qi-TAAR

24. One-way ticket - ذهاب ت ذكرة (Tadhkirah dhahāb)

- Sound Intonation: tad-KHEE-rah dha-HAAB

25. Round-trip ticket - وعودة ذهاب ت ذكرة (Tadhkirah dhahāb wa-ʿūdah)

- Sound Intonation: tad-KHEE-rah dha-HAAB wa-ʿOO-dah

26. Platform Number - المنصة رقم (Raqm al-manshah)

- Sound Intonation: ra-QAM al-man-SHAH

27. Waiting Area - الان تظار منطقة (Munṭaqah al-intiẓār)

- Sound Intonation: mun-TA-qah al-in-TIZ-aar

28. Commute - ال يومي الان تقال (Al-intiqāl al-yawmi)

- Sound Intonation: al-in-TI-qal al-ya-WA-mee

29. Metro Map - ال مـ ترو طةخري (Khariṭah al-mitrū)

- Sound Intonation: kha-REE-tah al-mee-TRO

30. Fare Card - ت ذكرة بـ طاقة (Biṭāqah tadhkirah)

- Sound Intonation: bi-TAA-qah tad-KHEE-rah

31. Transit System - ال عام ال نقل ن ظام (Naẓām an-naql al-ʿāmah)

- Sound Intonation: na-ZAAM an-na-ql al-ʿAA-mah

32. Bus Terminal - ال حاف لات محطة (Maḥṭah al-ḥāfilāt)

- Sound Intonation: maḥ-TAH al-ha-FEE-lat

33. Subway Station - الم ترو محطة (Maḥṭah al-mitrū)

- Sound Intonation: maḥ-TAH al-mee-TRO

34. Rush Hour - ساعات الذروة (Sā'āt adh-dhurwah)

- Sound Intonation: saa-AAT adh-dhu-RAW-wah

35. Monthly Pass - شهري ت صريح (Taṣrīḥ shahri)

- Sound Intonation: ta-SREEḤ sha-HREE

These words and phrases will be helpful when using public transport and navigating transportation systems in Arabic-speaking regions. Practice the sound intonations to ensure clear communication during your travels.

Renting a Car

Here are some common words and phrases related to renting a car in Arabic, along with their English translations and sound intonations:

1. Rent a Car - سـ يارة جارا سـ تئ (Isti'jār sayyārah)

Sound Intonation: is-ti-JAAR sa-yaa-RAH

2. Car Rental Agency - ت أجـ ير وكـ الـة الـ سـ يارات (Wakālah ta'jīr as-sayyārāt)

Sound Intonation: wa-KAA-lah ta-A-jir al-sa-YAA-raat

3. Reservation - حجز (Ḥajz)

Sound Intonation: ḥajz

4. Rental Agreement - اتّ فاق ية الإي جار (Ittifāqiyat al-ījār)

Sound Intonation: i-ti-FAA-qee-yat al-i-JAAR

5. Driver's License - رخ صة ال ق يادة (Rukhsah al-qiyādah)

Sound Intonation: rookh-SAH al-kee-YAA-dah

6. Insurance - تأ م ين (Taʾmīn)

Sound Intonation: ta-A-meem

7. Fuel/Gasoline - وق ود (Waqūd)

Sound Intonation: wa-QOOD

8. Mileage - عداد ال مساف ة (ʿadad al-masāfah)

Sound Intonation: ʿa-DAD al-ma-SA-fah

9. Drop-off Location - موقع الـ تسـ لـيم (Mawqīʿ at-taslīm)

Sound Intonation: maw-KEEʿ at-tas-LEEM

10. Pick-up Location - موقع الا سـ تلام (Mawqīʿ al-istilām)

- Sound Intonation: maw-KEEʿ al-is-tee-LAAM

11. Car Model - نموذج الـ سـ يارة (Namūḏaj as-sayyārah)

- Sound Intonation: na-MOO-thal al-sa-YAA-ra

12. Rental Period - فـ تر ة الإيـ جار (Fatrah al-ījār)

- Sound Intonation: fat-RAH al-i-JAAR

13. Vehicle Condition - حالة السيارة (Ḥālah as-sayyārah)

- Sound Intonation: ha-LAH al-sa-YAA-rah

14. Car Key - مفتاح السيارة (Miftāḥ as-sayyārah)

- Sound Intonation: mif-TAAḥ al-sa-YAA-rah

15. Rental Rate - سعر الإيجار (Saʿr al-ījār)

- Sound Intonation: sa-AR al-i-JAAR

16. GPS Navigation - تصفح GPS (Taṣafaḥ GPS)

- Sound Intonation: tas-FAH GPS

17. Rental Office - مكتب التأجير (Maktab at-taʾjīr)

- Sound Intonation: mak-TAB at-ta-A-jeer

18. Full Tank - ممتلئ خزان (Khuzaan mumtali')

- Sound Intonation: khu-ZAAN mum-ta-LEE'

19. Compact Car - صغيرة سيارة (Sayyārah ṣaghīrah)

- Sound Intonation: sa-yaa-RAH sa-GHEE-rah

20. Rental Car Insurance - سيارة تأمين الإيجار (Ta'mīn sayyārah al-ījār)

- Sound Intonation: ta-A-meen sa-yaa-RAH al-i-JAAR

These words and phrases will be helpful when renting a car and dealing with car rental agencies in Arabic-speaking regions.

Airport Vocabulary

Here are some common words and phrases related to airports in Arabic, along with their English translations and sound intonations:

1. Airport - مطار (Maṭār)

Sound Intonation: ma-TAAR

2. Terminal - ال مساف رين م ب نى (Mabnā al-musāfirīn)

Sound Intonation: ma-BNAH al-mu-SAA-fi-reen

3. Departures - ال مغادرة (Al-mughādarah)

Sound Intonation: al-mu-ghaa-DAR-ah

4. Arrivals - ال و صول (Al-wuṣūl)

Sound Intonation: al-wu-SOOL

5. Baggage Claim - الأم تعة اس تلام (Istilām al-umṭiʿah)

Sound Intonation: is-ti-LAAM al-um-TIʿ-ah

6. Check-in Counter - ت سجيل مك تب ال و صول (Maktab tasjīl al-wuṣūl)

Sound Intonation: mak-TAB tas-JEEL al-wu-SOOL

7. Boarding Pass - ال صعود ب طاقة (Biṭāqah al-ṣuʿūd)

Sound Intonation: bi-TAA-qah al-ṣu-OO-d

8. Security Check - الأمان ف حص (Faḥṣ al-amān)

Sound Intonation: fahṣ al-a-MAAN

9. Passport Control - ال سـ فر جواز مراق بة (Muraqabah jawāz as-safar)

Sound Intonation: mu-ra-QA-bah ja-WAAZ al-sa-FAR

10. Customs - ال جمارك (Al-jumārik)

- Sound Intonation: al-ju-MAAR-ik

11. Baggage Carousel - الأمـ تـعة سـ ير (Sīr al-umṭiʿah)

- Sound Intonation: seer al-um-TIʿ-ah

12. Airport Lounge - ال مـطار صالة (Ṣālah al-maṭār)

- Sound Intonation: ṣaa-LAH al-ma-TAAR

13. Gate - بـ وابـ ة (Bawābah)

- Sound Intonation: baw-AH-bah

14. Announcement - إعلان (Iʿlān)

- Sound Intonation: i-ʿLAAN

15. Flight - جوية رحلة (Riḥlah jawiyyah)

- Sound Intonation: ri-HLAH jo-WEE-yah

16. Airline - طيران شركة (Sharikat ṭayyirān)

- Sound Intonation:

Arrivals and Departures

Here are some words and phrases related to arrivals and departures at an airport in Arabic, along with their English translations and sound intonations:

Arrivals - الو صول (Al-wuṣūl)

Sound Intonation: al-wu-SOOL

Departures - الـمغادرة (Al-mughādarah)

Sound Intonation: al-mu-ghaa-DAR-ah

Flight - رحـ لة (Riḥlah)

Sound Intonation: ri-HLAH

Flight Number - رقم الرحلة (Raqm ar-riḥlah)

Sound Intonation: ra-QAM ar-ri-HLAH

Gate - بوابة (Bawābah)

Sound Intonation: baw-AH-bah

Boarding Pass - بطاقة الصعود (Biṭāqah al-ṣuʿūd)

Sound Intonation: bi-TAA-qah al-ṣu-OO-d

Passenger - مسافر (Musāfir)

Sound Intonation: mu-SAA-feer

Luggage - أمتعة (Umtiʿah)

Sound Intonation: um-TIʿ-ah

Baggage Claim - استلام الأمتعة (Istilām al-umtiʿah)

Sound Intonation: is-ti-LAAM al-um-TIʿ-ah

Customs - الجمارك (Al-jumārik)

Sound Intonation: al-ju-MAAR-ik

Passport Control - مراقبة جواز السفر (Muraqabah jawāz as-safar)

Sound Intonation: mu-ra-QA-bah ja-WAAZ al-sa-FAR

Immigration - الهجرة (Al-hijrah)

Sound Intonation: al-hi-JRAH

Security Check - فحص الأمان (Faḥṣ al-amān)

Sound Intonation: fahṣ al-a-MAAN

Airport Lounge - صالة المطار (Ṣālah al-maṭār)

Sound Intonation: ṣaa-LAH al-ma-TAAR

Baggage Carousel - سير الأمتعة (Sīr al-umṭiʿah)

Sound Intonation: seer al-um-TIʿ-ah

These words and phrases will be helpful when navigating an airport and communicating with airport staff in Arabic-speaking regions.

Practice the sound intonations to ensure clear communication during your travels.

Dining and Food

Here are some common words and phrases related to ordering food in Arabic, along with their English translations and sound intonations:

1. Menu - قائمة الطعام (Qā'imah al-ṭaʿām)

Sound Intonation: qa-AI-mah al-ta-AAM

2. Table - طاولة (Ṭawilah)

Sound Intonation: ṭa-AO-li-lah

3. Waiter - نادل (Nādil)

Sound Intonation: naa-DEL

4. Waitress - نادلة (Nādilah)

Sound Intonation: naa-DEE-lah

5. Order - ط لب (Ṭalab)

Sound Intonation: ṭa-LAB

6. Appetizer - مق ـبلات (Muqabilaat)

Sound Intonation: mu-ka-BI-laat

7. Main Course - ط بق ال رئ يسي (At-ṭabq ar-raʾīsī)

Sound Intonation: al-ta-BAK ar-ra-I-see

8. Dessert - ح لوى (Ḥalwah)

Sound Intonation: ḥal-WAAH

9. Drink - م شروب (Mashrub)

Sound Intonation: mash-ROOB

10. Water - ماء (Māʾ)

- Sound Intonation: ma-AH

11. Soda - غازي م شروب (Mashrub ghāzī)

- Sound Intonation: mash-ROOB ghaa-ZEE

12. Coffee - ق هوة (Qahwah)

- Sound Intonation: qa-HWAAH

13. Tea - شاي (Shāy)

- Sound Intonation: sha-AY

14. Breakfast - إف طار (Iftār)

- Sound Intonation: if-TAAR

15. Lunch - غداء (Ghaddā')

- Sound Intonation: gha-DAAH

16. Dinner - ع شاء ('Ashā')

- Sound Intonation: 'a-SHAA

17. I would like to order... - أرغب في ط لب... (Urghib fī ṭalab...)

- Sound Intonation: ur-GHIB fee ṭa-LAB...

18. What do you recommend? - ماذا تـوصى بـ ال ط لب؟ (Mādhā tusaī bāṭ-ṭalab?)

- Sound Intonation: ma-DHA too-SAI baṭ-ṭa-LAB?

19. Can I have the bill, please? - هل ي مكـنـ ني ال ح صول ع لى ال فاتـ ورة من ف ضلك؟ (Hal yumkinuni al-ḥuṣūl ʿalā al-fātūrah min faḍlik?)

- Sound Intonation: hal yoom-ki-NU-nee al-hu-SOOL ʿa-LA al-faa-TOO-rah min fa-DLIK?

20. I'm a vegetarian - أنا نباتي (Anā nabātī)

- Sound Intonation: a-NA na-baa-TEE

21. Appetizer - مقبلة (Muqabila)

- Sound Intonation: mu-qa-BEE-la

22. Soup - شوربة (Shūrbah)

- Sound Intonation: shoor-BAH

23. Salad - سلطة (Salata)

- Sound Intonation: sa-LAA-tah

24. Sandwich - ساندويتش (Sandweech)

- Sound Intonation: san-doo-WEETCH

25. Steak - شريحة لحم (Sharīḥah laḥm)

- Sound Intonation: sha-REE-hah LA-ham

26. Chicken - دجاج (Dajāj)

- Sound Intonation: da-JAAJ

27. Fish - سمك (Samak)

- Sound Intonation: sa-MAK

28. Vegetables - خ ضروات (Khudrawat)

- Sound Intonation: khud-ROA-wat

29. Fruits - ف واك ه (Fawākih)

- Sound Intonation: fa-WAA-kih

30. Spicy - حار (Ḥār)

- Sound Intonation: haar

31. Mild - ل ط يف (Laṭīf)

- Sound Intonation: la-TEEF

32. Well-done - مُطهَّر (Muṭahhar)

- Sound Intonation: mu-tah-HAR

33. Rare - نادر (Nādir)

- Sound Intonation: naa-DIR

34. Check, please - ف ضلك من الحساب، (Al-ḥisāb, min faḍlik)

- Sound Intonation: al-ḥi-SAAB, min fa-ḍlik

35. Can I get a doggy bag? - ي مكن ني هل ل ل باقي ؟ ك يس ع لى الحصول (Hal yumkinuni al-ḥuṣūl ʿalā kīs lil-bāqī?)

- Sound Intonation: hal yoom-ki-NU-nee al-hu-SOOL ʿa-LA kees lil-baa-QEE?

36. Bill/Check - ف ات ورة (Fātūrah)

- Sound Intonation: faa-TOO-rah

37. Tip - بـ قـشـ يش (Baqsheesh)

- Sound Intonation: baq-SHEESH

38. What's the special today? - ما هو الـ طـ بق الـ يومي ؟ (Mā huwa at-ṭabq al-yawmī?)

- Sound Intonation: ma HOO-wa at-TABQ al-ya-WA-mee?

39. I'm allergic to... - لدي حـسا سـ ية تـ جا ه... (Ladī ḥasāsīyah tijāh...)

- Sound Intonation: la-DEE ḥa-SA-see-yah ti-JAAH...

40. Can I have the menu, please? - هل يـ مـكـنـ ني الـحـصول عـ لى الـ قائـمة من فـ ضـلك؟ (Hal yumkinuni al-ḥuṣūl ʿalā al-qā'imah min faḍlik?)

- Sound Intonation: hal yoom-ki-NU-nee al-hu-SOOL ʿa-LA al-qa-AI-mah min fa-ḍlik?

These words and phrases will be useful when ordering food in Arabic-speaking restaurants.

Dining Out Phrases

Here are some words and phrases related to dining out in Arabic, along with their English translations and sound intonations:

1. Restaurant - مطعم (Maṭʿam)

Sound Intonation: ma-TAAM

2. Reservation - حجز (Ḥajz)

Sound Intonation: ḥajz

3. Table - طاول ة (Ṭawilah)

Sound Intonation: ṭa-AO-li-lah

4. Menu - ال طعام قائ مة (Qā'imah al-ṭaʿām)

Sound Intonation: qa-AI-mah al-ta-AAM

5. Waiter - نادل (Nādil)

Sound Intonation: naa-DEL

6. Waitress - نادلة (Nādilah)

Sound Intonation: naa-DEE-lah

7. Order - ط لب (Ṭalab)

Sound Intonation: ṭa-LAB

8. Menu - ال طعام قائ مة (Qā'imah al-ṭaʿām)

Sound Intonation: qa-AI-mah al-ta-AAM

9. Appetizer - مق بلات (Muqabilaat)

Sound Intonation: mu-ka-BI-laat

10. Main Course - ال رئ يسي ال ط بق (At-ṭabq ar-raʾīsī)

- Sound Intonation: al-ta-BAK ar-ra-I-see

11. Dessert - حـ لوى (Ḥalwah)

- Sound Intonation: ḥal-WAAH

12. Drink - مـ شروب (Mashrub)

- Sound Intonation: mash-ROOB

13. Water - ماء (Mā’)

- Sound Intonation: ma-AH

14. Wine - نـ بـ يذ (Nabeedh)

- Sound Intonation: na-BEEDH

15. Bill/Check - فـ اتـ ورة (Fātūrah)

- Sound Intonation: faa-TOO-rah

16. Tip - بـ قـ شـ يش (Baqsheesh)

- Sound Intonation: baq-SHEESH

17. I would like to order... - أرغب في طلب... (Urghib fī ṭalab...)

- Sound Intonation: ur-GHIB fee ṭa-LAB...

18. What's the special today? - ما هو الطبق اليومي؟ (Mā huwa at-ṭabq al-yawmī?)

- Sound Intonation: ma HOO-wa at-TABQ al-ya-WA-mee?

19. Can I get the bill, please? - هل يمكنني الحصول على الفاتورة من فضلك؟ (Hal yumkinuni al-ḥuṣūl ʿalā al-fātūrah min faḍlik?)

- Sound Intonation: hal yoom-ki-NU-nee al-hu-SOOL ʿa-LA al-faa-TOO-rah min fa-ḍlik?

20. Cheers! - صحة (Sihah)

- Sound Intonation: see-HA

Shopping for Groceries

Here are some words and phrases related to shopping for groceries in Arabic, along with their English translations and sound intonations:

1. Grocery Store - ب قالة م تجر (Matjar baqālah)

Sound Intonation: mat-JAR ba-QAA-lah

2. Shopping - ال تسوق (At-taswīq)

Sound Intonation: at-ta-SWEEK

3. Basket - س لة (Sallāh)

Sound Intonation: sal-LAAH

4. Cart/Trolley - عربة تسوق ('arbah tasswq)

Sound Intonation: 'ar-BAH tas-SWOK

5. Grocery List - قائمة البقالة (Qā'imah al-baqālah)

Sound Intonation: qa-AI-mah al-ba-QAA-lah

6. Aisle - ممر (Mamr)

Sound Intonation: mamr

7. Produce Section - قسم الخضروات (Qism al-khudrawat)

Sound Intonation: qis-M al-khud-ra-WAT

8. Dairy Section - قسم الألبان (Qism al-albān)

Sound Intonation: qis-M al-al-BAA-n

9. Meat Section - قسم اللحوم (Qism al-luḥūm)

Sound Intonation: qis-M al-lu-HOOM

10. Canned Goods - السلع المعلبة (As-silʿ al-maʿlabah)

- Sound Intonation: as-SILʿ al-ma-ʿla-BAH

11. Bread - خبز (Khubz)

- Sound Intonation: khubz

12. Milk - حليب (Ḥalīb)

- Sound Intonation: ḥa-LEEB

13. Eggs - بيض (Bayḍ)

- Sound Intonation: baiḍ

14. Fruits - فواكه (Fawākih)

- Sound Intonation: fa-WAA-kih

15. Vegetables - خ ضروات (Khudrawat)

- Sound Intonation: khud-ROA-wat

16. Meat - ل حم (Laḥm)

- Sound Intonation: LA-ham

17. Fish - سمك (Samak)

- Sound Intonation: sa-MAK

18. Cheese - ج ب نة (Jubnah)

- Sound Intonation: jib-NAH

19. Frozen Foods - ال مجمدة الأط عمة (Al-aṭʿamah al-majmudah)

- Sound Intonation: al-a-TA-mah al-maj-MOO-dah

20. Checkout Counter - كا ش ير (Kāshir)

- Sound Intonation: ka-SHEER

21. Receipt - إيصال (Iṣāl)

- Sound Intonation: i-SAAL

22. Discount - خصم (Khusum)

- Sound Intonation: khoo-SUM

23. Cash - نقداً (Naqdan)

- Sound Intonation: naq-DAN

24. Credit Card - بطاقة ائتمان (Biṭāqah i'timaan)

- Sound Intonation: bi-TAA-qah i'-ti-MAAN

25. Shopping Cart - سلة التسوق (Sallat at-taswīq)

- Sound Intonation: sal-LAT at-ta-SWEEK

26. Price - السعر (As-si'r)

- Sound Intonation: al-si-AAR

27. Sale - تخفيض (Takhfiẓ)

- Sound Intonation: takh-FEEZ

28. Brand - علامة تجارية (ʿālamah tijārīyah)

- Sound Intonation: ʿa-la-MAH ti-ja-REE-yah

29. Shopping Bag - حقيبة التسوق (Ḥaqībah at-taswīq)

- Sound Intonation: ḥa-QEE-bah at-ta-SWEEK

30. Checkout Line - صف الدفع (Ṣaff ad-dafʿ)

- Sound Intonation: ṣaf ad-daf

These words and phrases will help you when shopping for groceries in Arabic-speaking regions. Practice the sound intonations to communicate effectively while shopping.

Buying Food at the Market

1. Market - سوق (Sūq)

Sound Intonation: sooq

2. Vendor/Seller - بائع (Bāʾi)

Sound Intonation: baa-ee

3. Fresh - طازج (Ṭāzij)

Sound Intonation: ṭaa-ZAJ

4. Price - السعر (As-siʿr)

Sound Intonation: al-si-AAR

5. Quantity - كمية (Kamiyah)

Sound Intonation: ka-MEE-yah

6. Weight - وزن (Wazn)

Sound Intonation: wazn

7. Kilogram - كيلوغرام (Kīlūgram)

Sound Intonation: kee-lo-GRAAM

8. Gram - جرام (Jirām)

Sound Intonation: ji-RAAM

9. Pound - رطل (Ratl)

Sound Intonation: ra-TAL

10. Do you have...? - هل لديك...؟ (Hal ladayka...?)

- Sound Intonation: hal la-DAY-ka...?

11. I would like to buy... - أود شراء... (Awadu shira...)

- Sound Intonation: aw-wa-DOO she-RAA...

12. How much is this? - بكم هذا؟ (Bikam hadha?)

- Sound Intonation: bi-KAM ha-DHA?

13. Bargain - تفاوض (Tafaawuḍ)

- Sound Intonation: ta-fa-AW-dh

14. Quality - جودة (Jūdah)

- Sound Intonation: joo-DAH

15. Fresh Produce - منتجات طازجة (Muntajat ṭāzijah)

- Sound Intonation: mun-ta-JAT ṭaa-ZEE-jah

16. Fruit - فاكهة (Fākhhah)

- Sound Intonation: faa-KHAH

17. Vegetable - خضار (Khudhār)

- Sound Intonation: khud-HAAR

18. Meat - ل حم (Laḥm)

- Sound Intonation: LA-ham

19. Fish - سمك (Samak)

- Sound Intonation: sa-MAK

20. Bread - خ بز (Khubz)

- Sound Intonation: khubz

21. Cheese - ب نةج (Jubnah)

- Sound Intonation: jib-NAH

22. Eggs - ب يض (Bayḍ)

- Sound Intonation: baiḍ

23. Milk - ح ل يب (Ḥalīb)

- Sound Intonation: ḥa-LEEB

24. Butter - زب دة (Zubdah)

- Sound Intonation: zub-DAH

25. Sugar - سكر (Sukkar)

- Sound Intonation: soo-KAR

26. Salt - م لح (Milḥ)

- Sound Intonation: mil-H

27. Spices - ت وابـ ل (Tawābil)

- Sound Intonation: ta-WAA-beel

28. Can I taste it? - ت جرب ته؟ ي مكن ني هل (Hal yumkinuni tajribatuhu?)

- Sound Intonation: hal yoom-ki

29. Shopping Bag - ال تسوق حقيبة (Ḥaqībat at-taswīq)

- Sound Intonation: ḥa-QEE-bah at-ta-SWEEK

30. Cash - نقدًا (Naqdan)

- Sound Intonation: naq-DAN

31. Credit Card - ائ تمان ب طاقة (Biṭāqah i'timaan)

- Sound Intonation: bi-TAA-qah i'-ti-MAAN

32. Wallet - مح فظة (Muḥfaẓah)

- Sound Intonation: muḥ-fa-ZAH

33. Receipt - إي صال (Iṣāl)

- Sound Intonation: i-SAAL

34. Shopping List - ال تسوق قائ مة (Qā'imah at-taswīq)

- Sound Intonation: qa-AI-mah at-ta-SWEEK

35. Sale - تـ خـ فـ يض (Takhfiẓ)

- Sound Intonation: takh-FEEZ

36. Price Tag - بـ طاقة الـ سعر (Biṭāqah as-si‘r)

- Sound Intonation: bi-TAA-qah as-si-AAR

37. Organic - عـ ضوي (‘uḍwī)

- Sound Intonation: ‘uḍ-WEE

38. Non-GMO - خالي من الـ تعديل الـ وراثي (Khālī min at-ta‘dīl al-warithī)

- Sound Intonation: khā-LEE min at-ta-‘a-DHEEL al-wa-REE-thee

39. Shelf - رف (Raf)

- Sound Intonation: raf

40. Shopping Cart - ال تسوق عربة ('arbat at-taswīq)

- Sound Intonation: 'ar-BAH at-ta-SWEEK

41. Checkout Line - الدف ع صف (Ṣaff ad-daf')

- Sound Intonation: ṣaf ad-daf

42. Shopping Center - ت سوق مركز (Markaz taswīq)

- Sound Intonation: mar-KAZ tas-WEEK

43. Buy One, Get One Free - واحد ا شتر مجانًا واحد ع لى واحصل (Ishtar wāḥid waḥṣil 'alā wāḥid majānan)

- Sound Intonation: ish-TAR waa-HEED wa-HSIL 'a-LAA waa-HEED ma-JAA-nan

44. Shopping Mall - ت جاري مركز (Markaz tijārī)

- Sound Intonation: mar-KAZ ti-JAA-ree

45. Special Offer - خاص عرض (ʿarḍ khāṣ)

- Sound Intonation: ʿard khaas

46. Shopping Hours - ال تسوق ساعات (Sāʿāt at-taswīq)

- Sound Intonation: saa-ʿaat at-ta-SWEEK

47. Shopping Experience - ال تسوق ت جربة (Tajribat at-taswīq)

- Sound Intonation: ta-jri-BAT at-ta-SWEEK

48. Sale Price - ال بيع سعر (Siʿr al-bayʿ)

- Sound Intonation: siʿr al-bayʿ

49. Shopping District - ال تسوق م نطقة (Munṭaqah at-taswīq)

- Sound Intonation: mun-ṭa-QAH at-ta-SWEEK

50. Cashier - ال صندوق أم ين (Amin as-sandūq)

- Sound Intonation: a-MEEN as-san-DOOK

Words Relating to Hotel and Accommodations

Here are some words and phrases related to hotels and accommodations in Arabic, along with their English translations and sound intonations:

1. Hotel - ف ندق (Fanduq)

Sound Intonation: fan-DUQ

2. Room - غرف ة (Ghurfah)

Sound Intonation: ghur-FAH

3. Reservation - حجز (Ḥajz)

Sound Intonation: ḥajz

4. Reception - الا س تق بال (Al-istaqbal)

Sound Intonation: al-is-taq-BAL

5. Check-in - الوصول تسجيل (Tasjīl al-wuṣūl)

Sound Intonation: tas-JEEL al-wu-SOOL

6. Check-out - الخروج تسجيل (Tasjīl al-khurūj)

Sound Intonation: tas-JEEL al-khu-ROOJ

7. Key Card - المفتاح بطاقة (Biṭāqah al-miftāḥ)

Sound Intonation: bi-TAA-qah al-mif-TAAH

8. Single Room - منفردة غرفة (Ghurfah munfaridah)

Sound Intonation: ghur-FAH mun-fa-REE-dah

9. Double Room - مزدوجة غرفة (Ghurfah mazdujah)

Sound Intonation: ghur-FAH maz-du-JAH

10. Suite - جناح (Janah)

- Sound Intonation: ja-NAH

11. Reservation Confirmation - الحجز تأكيد (Taʾkīd al-ḥajz)

- Sound Intonation: ta-A-keed al-ḥajz

12. Room Service - الغرفة خدمة (Khidmat al-ghurfah)

- Sound Intonation: khid-MAT al-ghur-FAH

13. Hotel Staff - الفندق موظفو (Mawzufo al-fanduq)

- Sound Intonation: maw-ZOO-fo al-fan-DUQ

14. Reservation Desk - مكتب الحجز (Maktab al-ḥajz)

- Sound Intonation: mak-TAB al-ḥajz

15. Bellboy/Porter - حمال الأمتعة (Ḥamāl al-umṭiʿah)

- Sound Intonation: ḥa-MAAL al-um-TIʿ-ah

16. Lobby - اللوبي (Al-lūbī)

- Sound Intonation: al-LOO-bee

17. Receptionist - موظف الاستقبال (Mawzuf al-istaqbal)

- Sound Intonation: maw-ZOOF al-is-taq-BAL

18. Wi-Fi - واي فاي (Wāy fāy)

- Sound Intonation: wa-ee FA-ee

19. Towel - منشفة (Manṣafah)

- Sound Intonation: man-SHA-fah

20. Bed - سرير (Sirīr)

- Sound Intonation: se-REER

21. Pillow - وسادة (Wusādah)

- Sound Intonation: wa-SA-dah

22. Blanket - بطانية (Biṭānīyah)

- Sound Intonation: bi-TAA-nee-yah

23. Bathroom - حمام (Ḥamām)

- Sound Intonation: ḥa-MAAM

24. Shower - دش (Dush)

- Sound Intonation: duSH

25. Air Conditioning - ال هواء ت ك ي يف (Takyeef al-hawa')

- Sound Intonation: ta-kee-YE-f al-ha-WAA

26. Hotel Amenities - ال فندق مراف ق (Muraafaq al-fanduq)

- Sound Intonation: mu-RA-faq al-fan-DUQ

27. Breakfast Included - إف طار وج بة م تضمنة (Wajbah ifṭaar mutaḍamminah)

- Sound Intonation: waj-BAH if-TAAR mu-ta-ḍam-mi-NAH

28. Do Not Disturb - لا تُزعج (Lā tuzʿaj)

- Sound Intonation: laa tu-ZAAJ

29. Maid/Cleaning Service - ال تنظيف خدمة (Khidmat at-tanẓīf)

- Sound Intonation: khid-MAT at-tan-ZEEF

30. Mini-Bar - ال صغير ال بار (Al-baar as-ṣaghīr)

- Sound Intonation: al-BAAR as-ṣa-GHEER

These words and phrases will be helpful when checking in and staying at hotels in Arabic-speaking regions. Practice the sound intonations to ensure a comfortable and enjoyable stay.

Words Relating to Tourist Attractions

Here are some words and phrases related to tourist attractions in Arabic, along with their English translations and sound intonations:

1. Tourist Attractions - معالم سياحية (Maālim sayāḥiyyah)

Sound Intonation: ma-a-LIM sa-YAA-hee-yah

2. Landmarks - معالم (Maālim)

Sound Intonation: ma-AH-lim

3. Sightseeing - مشاهدة المعالم (Mushāhadah al-maālim)

Sound Intonation: mu-sha-HA-dah al-ma-a-LIM

4. Museum - م تحف (Mathaf)

Sound Intonation: ma-THEF

5. Art Gallery - ف نون صالة (Ṣālat funūn)

Sound Intonation: ṣa-LAHT fu-NOON

6. Historical Sites - ت اري خ ية مواق ع (Mawāqīʿ tārīkhiyyah)

Sound Intonation: ma-WAA-kee-ta-a-REE-ki-yyah

7. Monuments - ت ذكاري ة ن صب (Nuṣub tadhkāriyyah)

Sound Intonation: nu-SOOB tad-kha-REE-yah

8. Parks - حدائ ق (Ḥadā'iq)

Sound Intonation: ḥa-DA-a-eek

9. Zoo - حـ يوانات حديقة (Ḥadīqah ḥayawānāt)

Sound Intonation: ḥa-DEE-kah ḥa-yaw-a-NAAT

10. Aquarium - ال سمك حوض (Ḥawḍ as-samak)

- Sound Intonation: ḥawḍ as-sa-MAK

11. Botanical Garden - ن باتـ ية حديقة (Ḥadīqah nabātīyah)

- Sound Intonation: ḥa-DEE-kah na-baa-TEE-yah

12. Beach - شاطىء (Shāṭi’)

- Sound Intonation: sha-THEE

13. Mountains - ج بال (Jibāl)

- Sound Intonation: ji-BAL

14. Waterfall - شلال (Shalāl)

- Sound Intonation: sha-LAAL

15. Desert - صحراء (Ṣaḥrā')

- Sound Intonation: ṣa-HRAA

16. Forest - غاب ة (Ghābah)

- Sound Intonation: ghā-BAH

17. Historic Castle - ت اري خ ية ق لعة (Qalʿah tārīkhiyyah)

- Sound Intonation: qal-AH tah-REE-ki-yyah

18. National Park - وط ن ية حدي قة (Ḥadīqah waṭaniyyah)

- Sound Intonation: ḥa-DEE-kah wa-taa-NEE-yah

19. Tour Guide - سياحي مرشد (Murshid sayāḥi)

- Sound Intonation: mur-SHEED sa-YAA-hee

20. Admission Ticket - دخول تذكرة (Tadhkirat dukhūl)

- Sound Intonation: tad-khee-RAT du-khool

21. Landmark Statue - بارز تمثال (Timsāl bāriz)

- Sound Intonation: tim-SAAL BAA-riz

22. Scenic Viewpoint - مشاهدة نقطة (Nuqṭah mushāhadah)

- Sound Intonation: nuq-TAH mu-sha-HA-dah

23. Tourist Information - س ياح ية مع لومات (Maʿlūmāt sayāḥiyyah)

- Sound Intonation: ma-a-LOO-maat sa-YAA-hee-yah

24. Cultural Heritage Site - ال ترا ث موقع ال ثقافي (Mawqīʿ at-turāth ath-thaqāfī)

- Sound Intonation: maw-KEEʿ at-tu-RAATH ath-tha-QAA-fee

25. Souvenir Shop - ال تذكاري ة ال هداي ا م تجر (Majur al-hadāyā at-tadhkāriyyah)

- Sound Intonation: ma-TOOR al-ha-DAAY-a at-tad-kha-REE-yah

26. Tourist Map - س ياح ية خري طة (Khurayṭah sayāḥiyyah)

- Sound Intonation: khur-EE-tah sa-YAA-hee-yah

27. Tourist Information Center - مركز السياح معلومات (Markaz maʿlūmāt as-sayāḥ)

- Sound Intonation: mar-KAZ ma-a-LOO-maat as-sa-YAAH

28. Tourist Experience - سياحية تجربة (Tajribah sayāḥiyyah)

- Sound Intonation: ta-JREE-bah sa-YAA-hee-yah

29. Historical Landmarks - تاريخية معالم (Maālim tārīkhiyyah)

- Sound Intonation: ma-a-LEEM ta-a-REE-ki-yyah

30. Tourist Destination - سياحية وجهة

(Wajhah sayāḥiyyah)

- Sound Intonation: wa-JHAH sa-YAA-hee-yah

31. Amusement Park - ترفيهية مدينة

(Madīnat tarfīhiyah)

- Sound Intonation: ma-dee-NAT tar-fee-HEE-yah

32. Theme Park - ترفيهية حديقة

(Ḥadīqah tarfīhiyah)

- Sound Intonation: ḥa-dee-QAH tar-fee-HEE-yah

33. Adventure Park - مغامرات حديقة

(Ḥadīqah mughāmarāt)

- Sound Intonation: ḥa-dee-QAH moo-gha-MA-rat

34. Observatory - مرصد (Marsad)

- Sound Intonation: mar-SAD

35. Planetarium - مرصد فلكي (Marsad falakī)

- Sound Intonation: mar-SAD fa-LA-kee

36. Historical District - منطقة تاريخية (Munṭaqah tārīkhiyyah)

- Sound Intonation: mun-TA-qah ta-a-REE-ki-yyah

37. Natural Wonders - عجائب الطبيعة (ʿajāʾib at-ṭabīʿah)

- Sound Intonation: ʿa-JAA-ib at-ṭa-BEE-ah

38. Heritage Village - تراثية قرية (Qaryah turāthiyyah)

- Sound Intonation: qa-REE-yah tu-RA-thee-yyah

39. Historical Ruins - تاريخية آثار (Āthār tārīkhiyyah)

- Sound Intonation: ā-THAAR ta-a-REE-ki-yyah

40. Guided Tour - مرشدة جولة (Jawlat murshidah)

- Sound Intonation: joo-LAHT moor-SHEE-dah

41. Archaeological Site - أثري موقع (Mawqīʿ atharī)

- Sound Intonation: maw-KEEʿ a-THA-ree

42. Adventure Tourism - ال مغامرة سياحة (Sayāḥah al-mughāmarah)

- Sound Intonation: sa-YAA-hah al-moo-gha-MA-rah

43. Cultural Center - مركز ثقافي (Markaz thaqāfī)

- Sound Intonation: mar-KAZ tha-QAA-fee

44. Observatory Tower - ال مرصد برج (Burj al-marsad)

- Sound Intonation: burj al-mar-SAD

45. Scenic Route - سياحي طريق (Ṭarīq sayāḥī)

- Sound Intonation: ṭa-REEQ sa-YAA-hee

46. Famous Landmarks - معالم شهيرة (Maālim shahīrah)

- Sound Intonation: ma-a-LEEM sha-hee-RAH

47. Cultural Heritage Center - مركز التراث الثقافي (Markaz at-turāth ath-thaqāfī)

- Sound Intonation: mar-KAZ at-tu-RAATH ath-tha-QAA-fee

48. Art Installation - تثبيت فني (Tathbīt funī)

- Sound Intonation: tath-BEET foo-NEE

49. Interactive Exhibits - معروضات تفاعلية (Maʿrūḍāt tafāʿuliyyah)

- Sound Intonation: ma-a-ROO-daht ta-faa-oo-LEE-yah

50. Cultural Festival - مهرجان ثقافي (Mahrjaan thaqāfī)

- Sound Intonation: mah-ra-JAAN tha-QAA-fee

Emergency Situations

1. Hospital - مستشفى (Mustashfa)

Sound Intonation: mus-TASH-fa

2. Doctor - طبيب (Ṭabīb)

Sound Intonation: ṭa-BEEB

3. Nurse - ممرض / ممرضة (Mumarris / Mumarrisah)

Sound Intonation: mum-RESS / mum-RESS-ah

4. Patient - مريض (Mareeḍ)

Sound Intonation: ma-REEḌ

5. Emergency Room - غرفة الطوارئ (Ghurfat at-Tawari)

Sound Intonation: ghur-faht at-ta-WA-ree

6. Ambulance - إ سعاف (Isʿāf)

Sound Intonation: is-AAF

7. Pharmacy - صيدلية (Saydaliyah)

Sound Intonation: say-DA-lee-yah

8. Medication - دواء (Dawā)

Sound Intonation: da-WAA

9. Prescription - وصفة طبية (Wusfah Ṭibīyah)

Sound Intonation: wus-fah ṭi-BEE-yah

10. Health Insurance - تأمين صحي (Taʾmīn Ṣaḥī)

- Sound Intonation: ta-a-MEEN ṣa-HEE

11. Surgery - جراحة (Jarāḥah)

- Sound Intonation: ja-RAH-hah

12. X-ray - أشعة الأشعة السينية (Ashʿah as-Sīniyah)

- Sound Intonation: ash-ʿah as-si-NI-yah

13. Medical Examination - فحص طبي (Faḥṣ Ṭibī)

- Sound Intonation: fa-ḥs ṭi-BEE

14. Blood Pressure - ضغط الدم (Ḍaghṭ ad-Dam)

- Sound Intonation: ḍaghṭ ad-dam

15. Vaccination - تطعيم (Taṭʿīm)

- Sound Intonation: ta-ṭee-EM

16. Health Checkup - صحي ف حص (Faḥṣ Ṣaḥī)

- Sound Intonation: fa-ḥs ṣa-HEE

17. Medical Records - ط بية سجلات (Sijalat Ṭibīyah)

- Sound Intonation: si-JA-lat ṭi-BEE-yah

18. Waiting Room - الان تظار غرفة (Ghurfat al-Intiẓār)

- Sound Intonation: ghur-faht al-in-ti-ZAAR

19. Dentist - الأ سنان ط بيب (Ṭabīb al-Asnān)

- Sound Intonation: ṭa-BEEB al-as-NAAN

20. Surgery Room - الجراحة غرفة (Ghurfat al-Jarāḥah)

- Sound Intonation: ghur-faht al-ja-RAH-hah

21. Medical Equipment - طبية معدات (Muʿadāt Ṭibīyah)

- Sound Intonation: mu-ʿa-DAAT ṭi-BEE-yah

22. Health Specialist - صحي أخصائي (Akhuṣāʾī Ṣaḥī)

- Sound Intonation: akh-u-SAA-ee ṣa-HEE

23. Medical Staff - الطبيين العاملين (Al-ʿāmilīn aṭ-ṭibīyīn)

- Sound Intonation: al-ʿaa-MI-leen aṭ-ṭi-BEE-yin

24. Wheelchair - متحرك كرسي (Kursī mutaḥarrik)

- Sound Intonation: kur-SEE moo-ta-HAR-rik

25. Medical Test - ط بي اخ ة بار (Ikhtibār Ṭibī)

- Sound Intonation: ikh-ti-BAR ṭi-BEE

26. Health Center - صحي م ركز (Markaz Ṣaḥī)

- Sound Intonation: mar-KAZ ṣa-HEE

27. First Aid Kit - إ سعاف ع ل بة (ʿalabat isʿāf)

- Sound Intonation: ʿa-LA-bat is-AAF

28. Medical History - ال ط بي ال تاريخ (At-tārīkh aṭ-Ṭibī)

- Sound Intonation: at-taa-REEKH aṭ-ṭi-BEE

29. Emergency Contact - في الات صال جهة ال طوارئ حالات (Jihat al-ittiṣāl fī ḥalāt at-tawāri')

- Sound Intonation: ji-HA-tah al-i-ti-SAAL fee ha-LAT at-ta-WAA-ree

30. Health Examination - صحي ف حص (Faḥṣ Ṣaḥī)

- Sound Intonation: fa-ḥs ṣa-HEE

31. Health Insurance Card - ال تأم ين ب طاقة ال صحي (Biṭāqah at-Taʾmīn aṣ-Ṣaḥī)

- Sound Intonation: bi-TAA-qah at-ta-a-MEEN as-ṣa-HEE

32. Medical Condition - ط بية حالة (Ḥālah Ṭibīyah)

- Sound Intonation: ḥaa-LAH ṭi-BEE-yah

33. Medical Certificate - ط بية شهادة (Shahādah Ṭibīyah)

- Sound Intonation: sha-HAA-dah ṭi-BEE-yah

34. Specialist Doctor - م تخصص ط ب يب (Ṭabīb mutakhassiṣ)

- Sound Intonation: ṭa-BEEB moo-takh-ha-SEEṣ

35. Radiology - الأ شعة (Al-ʾAshʿah)

- Sound Intonation: al-aSH-a

36. Medical Examination Room - غرف ة فحص ال طبي ال (Ghurfat al-Faḥṣ aṭ-Ṭibī)

- Sound Intonation: ghur-FAT al-fa-ḥṣ aṭ-ṭi-BEE

37. Medical Specialist Appointment - موعد مع اخ تصاصي ط بي (Mawʿid maʿ ikhtisāṣi ṭibī)

- Sound Intonation: maw-EED maʿ ikh-ti-SA-see ṭi-BEE

38. Operating Room - غرفة العمليات (Ghurfat al-ʿamalīyāt)

- Sound Intonation: ghur-FAT al-ʿa-ma-LEE-yat

39. Health Checkup Package - باقة فحص صحي (Bāqat faḥṣ ṣaḥī)

- Sound Intonation: ba-AH-kat fa-ḥs ṣa-HEE

40. Medical Test Results - نتائج الاختبارات الطبية (Nataʾij al-ikhtibarāt aṭ-ṭibīyah)

- Sound Intonation: na-taa-IJ al-ikh-ti-ba-RAAT aṭ-ṭi-BEE-yah

41. Health History Form - استمارة التاريخ الصحي (Istamārah at-Tārīkh aṣ-Ṣaḥī)

- Sound Intonation: is-ta-MA-ra at-taa-REEKH as-ṣa-HEE

42. Intensive Care Unit (ICU) - وحدة العناية المركزة (Waḥdat al-ʿināyah al-markazah)

- Sound Intonation: wa-HDAT al-ʿi-naa-YAH al-mar-ka-ZAH

43. Health Insurance Policy - وثيقة التأمين الصحي (Wathīqat at-Taʾmīn aṣ-Ṣaḥī)

- Sound Intonation: wa-THEE-qat at-ta-a-MEEN as-ṣa-HEE

44. Medical Treatment - علاج طبي (ʿilāj Ṭibī)

- Sound Intonation: ʿi-LAAJ ṭi-BEE

45. Blood Test - الدم تحليل (Taḥlīl ad-Dam)

- Sound Intonation: ta-HLEE-l ad-dam

46. Health Records Department - قسم الصحية السجلات (Qism as-Sijalāt aṣ-Ṣaḥīyah)

- Sound Intonation: qisam as-si-jlaat as-ṣa-HEE-yah

47. Pediatrician - أطفال طبيب (Ṭabīb aṭfāl)

- Sound Intonation: ṭa-BEEB aṭ-faal

48. Health Assessment - صحي تقييم (Taqqīm Ṣaḥī)

- Sound Intonation: taq-KEEM ṣa-HEE

49. Medical Expenses - طبية نفقات (Nafaqat Ṭibīyah)

- Sound Intonation: na-FA-kat ṭi-BEE-yah

50. Medical Laboratory - ط بي مخ ت بر (Makhtabar Ṭibī)

- Sound Intonation: makh-ta-BAR ṭi-BEE

Reporting Incidents

1. Incident - حادث (Ḥādith)

Sound Intonation: ḥaa-DITH

2. Report - ت قري ر (Taqrīr)

Sound Intonation: taq-REER

3. Emergency - طوارئ حال ة (Ḥālat Ṭawāri)

Sound Intonation: ḥaa-LAT ṭa-WAA-ree

4. Police - ال شرط ة (Ash-Shurṭah)

Sound Intonation: ash-shur-TAH

5. Accident - مروري حادث (Ḥādith murūrī)

Sound Intonation: ḥaa-DITH mu-ROO-ree

6. Fire - حري ق (Ḥariq)

Sound Intonation: ḥa-REEQ

7. Theft - سرقة (Sariqah)

Sound Intonation: sa-REE-qah

8. Robbery - سطو مسلح (Suto musallah)

Sound Intonation: SOO-to moo-sa-LAH

9. Witness - شاهد (Shāhid)

Sound Intonation: sha-HID

10. Emergency Services - خدمات الطوارئ (Khidmat al-Ṭawāri)

- Sound Intonation: khid-MAT al-ṭa-WAA-ree

11. Call the Police - اتصل بالشرطة (Itaṣal bish-shurṭah)

- Sound Intonation: it-a-SAL be-shur-TAH

12. Call for Help - اتصل بالمساعدة (Itaṣal bial-musaʿadah)

- Sound Intonation: it-a-SAL be-al-mu-sa-a-DAH

13. Emergency Number - رقم الطوارئ (Raqm at-Ṭawāri)

- Sound Intonation: ra-QUM at-ṭa-WAA-ree

14. Accident Scene - موقع الحادث (Mawqīʿ al-Ḥādith)

- Sound Intonation: maw-KEEʿ al-ḥaa-DITH

15. Witness Statement - تصريح الشاهد (Taṣrīḥ ash-shāhid)

- Sound Intonation: ta-SREEḤ ash-shaa-HID

16. Emergency Response - اسـتجابـة الطوارئ (Istijābah al-Ṭawāri)

- Sound Intonation: is-ti-JAA-bah al-ṭa-WAA-ree

17. Crime Scene - موقـع الجريـمة (Mawqīʿ al-jarīmah)

- Sound Intonation: maw-KEEʿ al-ja-REE-mah

18. Call 911 - اتـصل بـرقم ٩١١ (Itaṣal biraqm 911)

- Sound Intonation: it-a-SAL bi-raqm tis-a-TAAH

19. Emergency Dispatch - إرسال الطوارئ (Irsāl al-Ṭawāri)

- Sound Intonation: ir-SAAL al-ṭa-WAA-ree

20. Incident Report Form - ت قري ر ن موذج ال حادث (Namūḏaj taqrīr al-ḥādith)

- Sound Intonation: na-moo-THAJ taq-reer al-ḥaa-DITH

21. Crime Investigation - في ال تحقيق ال جري مة (At-taḥqīq fī al-jarīmah)

- Sound Intonation: at-tah-KEEK fee al-ja-REE-mah

22. Emergency Alert - ال طوارئ ت ن ب يه (Tanbīh al-Ṭawāri)

- Sound Intonation: tan-BEEH al-ṭa-WAA-ree

23. Suspicious Activity - م ش بوه ن شاط (Nashaʿ mushbūh)

- Sound Intonation: NA-shaat mush-BOO-h

24. Rescue - إنقاذ (Inqāḏ)

- Sound Intonation: in-QAAZ

25. Disaster - كارثة (Kārithah)

- Sound Intonation: ka-REETH-ah

26. Emergency Plan - خطة الطوارئ (Khṭah al-Ṭawāri)

- Sound Intonation: kh-TAH al-ṭa-WAA-ree

27. Crime Prevention - منع الجريمة (Manaʿ al-jarīmah)

- Sound Intonation: ma-NA al-ja-REE-mah

28. Lost and Found - فقدان وعثور (Fuqdaan waʿthur)

- Sound Intonation: fuq-DAAN wa-a-THOOR

29. Search and Rescue - بحث الا نقاذ والإذ (Al-bahth wal-inqāḏ)

- Sound Intonation: al-bahth wal-in-QAAZ

30. Disaster Preparedness - الا س تعداد لـ لكوارث (Al-istaʿdād lil-kawārith)

- Sound Intonation: al-ista-AH-dad lil-ka-WAA-reeth

31. Security - أمان (Amān)

- Sound Intonation: a-MAAN

32. Suspicion - شك (Shakk)

- Sound Intonation: shak

33. Witness Protection - ال شاهد حماية (Ḥimāyah ash-Shāhid)

- Sound Intonation: ḥi-MAA-yah ash-shaa-HID

34. Crime Scene Investigation (CSI) - الجريمة موقع في التحقيق (At-taḥqīq fī mawqīʿ al-jarīmah)

- Sound Intonation: at-tah-KEEK fee maw-KEEʿ al-ja-REE-mah

35. Search Warrant - بتفتيش إذن (Idin bitfātīš)

- Sound Intonation: idh-in bit-faa-TEE-sh

36. Traffic Accident - مروري حادث (Ḥādith murūrī)

- Sound Intonation: ḥaa-DITH mu-ROO-ree

37. Emergency Response Team - فريق للطوارئ الاستجابة (Fariq al-istijābah lil-ṭawāriʾ)

- Sound Intonation: fa-REEQ al-is-ti-JAA-bah lil-ṭa-WAA-ree

38. Disaster Relief - ال كوارث مساعدات (Musaʿadāt al-kawārith)

- Sound Intonation: mu-saa-a-DAAT al-ka-WAA-reeth

39. Witness Testimony - ال شاهد شهادة (Shahādah ash-Shāhid)

- Sound Intonation: sha-HAA-dah ash-shaa-HID

40. Search Party - ال بحث فريق (Fariq al-bahth)

- Sound Intonation: fa-REEQ al-bahth

41. Emergency Contact Information - ال طوارئ حالات فى الاتـ صال جهة معلومات (Maʿlūmāt jihat al-ittiṣāl fī ḥalāt al-ṭawāriʾ)

- Sound Intonation: ma-a-loo-MAAT ji-HAH-ti al-i-ti-SAAL fee ha-LAT al-ṭa-WAA-ree

42. Police Station - ال شرطة مركز (Markaz ash-Shurṭah)

- Sound Intonation: mar-KAZ ash-shur-TAH

43. Missing Person - م فقود شخص (Shakhṣ mafqūd)

- Sound Intonation: shakhS maf-KOOD

44. Evacuation Plan - الإخلاء خطة (Khṭah al-ikhla)

- Sound Intonation: kh-TAH al-iKH-LAA

45. Search and Rescue Team - فريق البحث والإنقاذ (Fariq al-bahth wal-inqāḏ)

- Sound Intonation: fa-REEQ al-bahth wal-in-QAAZ

46. Emergency Alert System - نظام التنبيه في الحالات الطارئة (Naẓām at-tanbīh fī al-ḥalāt al-ṭāri'ah)

- Sound Intonation: na-ZAAM at-tan-BEE-h fee al-ha-LAAT al-ṭaa-REE-yah

47. Witness Protection Program - برنامج حماية الشهود (Barnāmaj ḥimāyat ash-shuhūd)

- Sound Intonation: bar-NAH-maj ḥi-MAA-yat ash-shoo-HOOD

48. Missing Child - م فقود ط فل (Ṭifl mafqūd)

- Sound Intonation: ṭifl maf-KOOD

49. Disaster Recovery - ال كوارث ا س تعادة (Istīʿādat al-kawārith)

- Sound Intonation: is-ti-aa-DAT al-ka-WAA-reeth

50. Emergency Evacuation Route - طري ق ال طارئ الإخ لاء (Ṭarīq al-ikhla al-ṭāri')

- Sound Intonation: ṭa-REEQ al-iKH-LAA al-ṭaa-REE-yah

Phrases Used in Social Interactions

Here are some words and phrases used in social interactions in Arabic, along with their English translations and sound intonations:

1. Conversation - محادثة (Muḥāḍaṭah)

Sound Intonation: mu-HAA-ḍa-tah

2. Friend - صديق (Ṣadīq)

Sound Intonation: ṣa-DEEK

3. Socialize - تواصل (Tawāṣul)

Sound Intonation: ta-WAA-ṣool

4. Greeting - تحية (Tahīyah)

Sound Intonation: ta-HEE-yah

5. Meet - اجتماع (Ijtimāʿ)

Sound Intonation: ij-ti-MAA

6. Invitation - دعوة (Daʿwah)

Sound Intonation: da-OO-ah

7. Gathering - تجمع (Tajammul)

Sound Intonation: ta-JAM-mool

8. Party - حفلة (Ḥaflah)

Sound Intonation: ḥaf-LAH

9. Host - مضيف (Muḍīf) / مضيفة (Muḍīfah)

Sound Intonation: mu-ḍeef / mu-ḍeefah

10. Guest - ضيف (Ḍayf)

- Sound Intonation: ḍayf

11. Celebration - احـ تـ فال (Iḥtifāl)

- Sound Intonation: iḥ-ti-FAAL

12. Toast - نـخب (Nukhb)

- Sound Intonation: nu-KHAB

13. Cheers! - صحة (Ṣaḥah)

- Sound Intonation: ṣa-ḥah

14. Introduction - تـ قديـم (Taqqadīm)

- Sound Intonation: taq-QA-deem

15. Small Talk - عابـ رة محادثـ ة (Muḥāḍaṭah ʿābirah)

- Sound Intonation: mu-HAA-ḍa-tah ʿaa-BEE-rah

16. Compliment - إعجاب (Iʿjāb)

- Sound Intonation: iʿ-JAAB

17. Goodbye - وداعًا (Wadāʿan)

- Sound Intonation: wa-DAA-an

18. Nice to meet you - سرر ت بـ لقائك (Sarartu biliqa'ik)

- Sound Intonation: sa-RAR-tu bi-li-QAA-ik

19. Apology - اع تذار (Iʿtizār)

- Sound Intonation: iʿ-ti-ZAAR

20. Thank you - شكرًا (Shukran)

- Sound Intonation: shuk-RAN

21. Please - من فضلك (Min faḍlik)

- Sound Intonation: min fa-ḍlik

22. Excuse me - عذرًا ('iḏran)

- Sound Intonation: 'iḏ-RAN

23. How are you? - كيف حالك؟ (Kayfa ḥāluk?)

- Sound Intonation: KAY-fa ḥaa-LUK?

24. I'm fine, thank you - أنا بخير، شكرًا (Ana bikhayr, shukran)

- Sound Intonation: A-na bi-KHA-yir, shuk-RAN

25. What's your name? - ما اسمك؟ (Mā ismak?)

- Sound Intonation: MAH is-MAK?

26. My name is [Name] - اسمي [اسم] (Ismi [Ism])

- Sound Intonation: IS-mee [Ism]

27. Where are you from? - أذ ت؟ أي ن من (Min ayna anta?)

- Sound Intonation: Min AY-n an-TA?

28. I'm from [Country] - [ال بـ لد] من أذ ا (Ana min [al-bald])

- Sound Intonation: A-na min [al-BALD]

29. Yes - ذ عم (Naʿam)

- Sound Intonation: na-ʿam

30. No - لا (Lā)

- Sound Intonation: LAA

31. Pleased to meet you - بـ لقائك سرر ت (Sarartu biliqa'ik)

- Sound Intonation: sa-RAR-tu bi-li-QAA-ik

32. Can I help you? - ب إمكاني هل مساعدتك؟ (Hal bi'umkani musa'idatuk?)

- Sound Intonation: HAL bi-u-MKA-nee mu-saa-i-DA-tuk?

33. Of course - ب ال ط بع (Bilṭab')

- Sound Intonation: bil-ṭab'

34. Congratulations - ت هان ينا (Tahanina)

- Sound Intonation: ta-HAA-nee-na

35. I'm sorry - آ سف (Asif) / آ سـ فة أنا (Ana asifah)

- Sound Intonation: AA-sif / A-na AA-si-fah

36. You're welcome - وال سعة ال رحب ع لى (ʿalā ar-raḥb wal-saʿah)

- Sound Intonation: ʿa-LAA ar-ra-HB wal-sa-AH

37. What's new? - ما الجديـد؟ (Ma al-jadid?)

- Sound Intonation: MAH al-ja-DEED?

38. How's your day? - كيف كان يومك؟ (Kayfa kān yawmak?)

- Sound Intonation: KAY-fa kaan ya-MAK?

39. Let's catch up - لنلتقي ونتحدث (Lanaltaqi wantuhaddith)

- Sound Intonation: lan-al-ta-QEE wan-tuhad-DITH

40. I don't understand - لا أفهم (Lā afham)

- Sound Intonation: LAA af-HAM

41. Can you repeat that? - هل يمكنك تكرار ذلك؟ (Hal yumkinuka takrar dhalik?)

- Sound Intonation: HAL yu-MKI-nu-ka tak-RAAR dha-LIK?

42. Nice weather today, isn't it? - الطقس جميل اليوم، أليس كذلك؟ (At-taqs jamīl alyawm, alaysa kadhalik?)

- Sound Intonation: at-taqS ja-MEEL al-yawm, alaysa ka-DHA-lik?

43. What do you do for a living? - ماذا تعمل في الحياة؟ (Mādhā taʿmal fī al-ḥayāh?)

- Sound Intonation: MAA-dha ta-AMAL fee al-HA-ya?

44. I'm a [Profession] - أنا [مهنة] (Ana [Mihnah])

- Sound Intonation: A-na [Mih-NAH]

45. How's your family? - كيف حال عائلتك؟ (Kayfa ḥāl ʿāʾilatak?)

- Sound Intonation: KAY-fa ḥaa-LU a-ee-la-TAK?

46. What's your hobby? - هوايـ تك؟ هو ما (Ma huwa hawāyatuk?)

- Sound Intonation: MA-ho HOO-wai-YA-tuk?

47. I enjoy [Hobby] - [هواية] بـ . ا سـ تمـ تع أنا (Ana istamtaʿ bi [Hawāyah])

- Sound Intonation: A-na is-tam-TAAʿ bi [Haw-WAI-yah]

48. Can I have your contact information? - معلومات على الحصول يمكنني هل اتـ صالك؟ (Hal yumkinuni al-ḥuṣūl ʿalā maʿlūmāt ittiṣālik?)

- Sound Intonation: HAL yu-MKI-nu-ni al-ḥu-SOOL ʿa-LAA ma-a-LOO-maat it-ti-SA-lik?

49. It's been a pleasure talking to you - كان من دواعي سروري الحديث معك (Kān min duwāʿi sarūrī al-ḥadīth maʿak)

- Sound Intonation: kaan min du-WAA-ee sa-ROO-ree al-ha-DEETH ma-ak

50. Take care - اعتني بنفسك (Iʿtani binafsik)

- Sound Intonation: iʿ-ta-NEE bee-NAF-sik

These additional words and phrases will help you navigate various social situations and conversations in Arabic. Practice the sound intonations for effective communication in social settings.

Expressing Interest

Here are some words and phrases used in expressing interest in Arabic, along with their English translations and sound intonations:

1. Interesting - ل لاه تمام م ث ير (Muthīr lil-ihtimām)

Sound Intonation: mu-THEER lil-ihti-MAAM

2. Fascinating - رائ ع (Rā'i')

Sound Intonation: ra-EE

3. Engaging - جذاب (Jaḏāb)

Sound Intonation: jad-DHAAB

4. Captivating - جذّاب (Jaḏḏāb)

Sound Intonation: jad-DHAAB

5. I'm interested - مهتم أنا (Ana muhtam)

Sound Intonation: A-na muh-TAM

6. Tell me more - قل لي المزيد (Qul lī al-mazīd)

Sound Intonation: qul LEE al-ma-ZEED

7. That's intriguing - ذلك مثير للاهتمام (Ẓalik muthīr lil-ihtimām)

Sound Intonation: ẓa-LIK mu-THEER lil-ihti-MAAM

8. I find it fascinating - أجده رائعًا (Ajidhu rāʾiʿan)

Sound Intonation: A-jid-HU ra-EE-an

9. I'm curious - أنا فضولي (Ana fuḍūlī)

Sound Intonation: A-na fu-ḍoo-LEE

10. That's impressive - مؤثر ذلك (Ẓalik mu'aṯṯir)

- Sound Intonation: ẓa-LIK mu-a-THIR

11. This caught my attention - لفت انتباهي هذا (Lafta intibāhī hadā)

- Sound Intonation: laf-ta in-ti-BA-hi ha-DA

12. I'd like to know more about this - أود معرفة المزيد عن هذا (Awad maʿrifat al-mazīd ʿan hadā)

- Sound Intonation: A-wad ma-a-ri-FAT al-ma-ZEED ʿan ha-DA

13. Can you tell me about it? - هل يمكنك أن تخبرني عنه؟ (Hal yumkinuka an takhbirnī ʿanhu?)

- Sound Intonation: HAL yu-MKI-nu-ka an takh-BEER-nee ʿan-HU?

14. I'm eager to learn more - ع لى حريـ ص أنا الـمزيـد تـ عـلم (Ana ḥarīṣ ʿalā taʿallum al-mazīd)

- Sound Intonation: A-na ḥa-REEṣ ʿa-LAA ta-a-LUM al-ma-ZEED

15. I'm all ears - ل لا سـ تماع هـ نا أنا (Ana huna lil-istimāʿ)

- Sound Intonation: A-na hoo-NA lil-is-ti-MAA

16. Share more details - من الـمزيـد شارك الـ تـ فا صـ يل (Sharik al-mazīd min at-tafāsīl)

- Sound Intonation: sha-RIK al-ma-ZEED min at-ta-faa-SEEL

17. I'm keen on this topic - لـ هذا مـ تحمس أذا الـموضـوع (Ana mutaḥammis li-hādhā al-mawḍūʿ)

- Sound Intonation: A-na mu-ta-HAM-mis li-haa-DA al-maw-DOO

18. Please explain more - من فـضـلك، شرح الـمزيـد (Min faḍlik, sharḥ al-mazīd)

- Sound Intonation: min fa-ḍlik, sharḥ al-ma-ZEED

19. I'd love to hear about it - سأحب أن أسمع عـنها (Sa'uḥibu an asmaʿ ʿanha)

- Sound Intonation: sa-u-HI-bu an as-MA-a ʿan-HA

20. Can you give me more information? - هل يـمكنك أن تـعطيـني مزيدًا من الـمعلومات؟

(Hal yumkinuka an taʿṭīnī mazīdan min al-maʿlūmāt?)

- Sound Intonation: HAL yu-MKI-nu-ka an ta-ṭEE-nee ma-ZEE-dan min al-ma-a-LOO-maat?

21. That's exciting - م ث ير ذلك (Ẓalik muthīr)

- Sound Intonation: ẓa-LIK mu-THEER

22. I'm really into this - ب هذا حقًا م ه تم أنا (Ana muhtam ḥaqan bihadha)

- Sound Intonation: A-na muh-TAM ḥa-QAN bi-HA-da

23. I can't wait to learn more - أس تط يع لا ال مزيد ل معرفة الان تظار (Lā astaṭīʿ al-intiẓār limaʿrifat al-mazīd)

- Sound Intonation: LAA as-ta-TEEʿ al-in-TI-zaar li-ma-a-RI-fat al-ma-ZEED

24. I'm intrigued by this topic - مشوق أنا الموضوع ل هذا (Ana mashūq li-hādhā al-mawḍūʿ)

- Sound Intonation: A-na ma-SHOOQ li-haa-DA al-maw-DOO

25. What a fascinating idea! - رائعة فكرة! (Fikrah rāʾiʿah!)

- Sound Intonation: FIK-rah ra-EE-a!

26. I'm impressed - أعجبتني لقد (Laqad ʾaʿjabatnī)

- Sound Intonation: la-QAD ʾa-ʿja-BAT-nee

27. You have my attention - لديك انتباهي (Ladayka intibāhī)

- Sound Intonation: la-DAY-ka in-ti-BA-a-HEE

28. I'm really curious about this - أنا متحمس حقًا لهذا (Ana mutaḥammis ḥaqan lihādhā)

- Sound Intonation: A-na mu-ta-HAM-mis ḥa-QAN li-HAA-da

29. Tell me more, please - قل لي المزيد، من فضلك (Qul lī al-mazīd, min faḍlik)

- Sound Intonation: qul LEE al-ma-ZEED, min fa-ḍlik

30. This is really captivating - حقًا مذهل هذا (Hadā mudh-hil ḥaqan)

- Sound Intonation: ha-DA mudh-HIL ḥa-QAN

31. I'm all ears - أنا هنا للاستماع (Ana huna lil-istimāʿ)

- Sound Intonation: A-na hoo-NA lil-is-ti-MAA

32. Your explanation is quite interesting - شرحك مثير للاهتمام (Sharhuk muthīr lil-ihtimām)

- Sound Intonation: shar-HUK mu-THEER lil-ihti-MAAM

33. That's really thought-provoking - هذا يثير الفكر حقًا (Haḏā yuṯīr al-fikr ḥaqan)

- Sound Intonation: ha-DA yu-THEER al-fikr ḥa-QAN

34. I'm eager to explore this further - أنا حريص على استكشاف هذا بعمق (Ana ḥarīṣ ʿalā istikshāf hādhā biʿamaq)

- Sound Intonation: A-na ḥa-REEṣ ʿa-LAA is-tik-SHAAF haa-DA bi-ʿa-MAQ

35. Can you share more insights? - هل يمكنك مشاركة المزيد من الرؤى؟ (Hal yumkinuka mushārakat al-mazīd min al-ruʾā?)

- Sound Intonation: HAL yu-MKI-nu-ka mu-shaa-RAK-at al-ma-ZEED min al-ru-AH?

36. I can't get enough of this - لا يمكنني الاستغناء عن هذا (Lā yumkinunī al-istiġnāʾ ʿan hādhā)

- Sound Intonation: LAA yum-ki-NU-ni al-is-ti-GHNA-a ʿan haa-DA

37. That's truly captivating - جذاب حقًا ذلك (Ẓalik ḥaqan jaḏāb)

- Sound Intonation: ẓa-LIK ḥa-QAN ja-DHAAB

38. I'm completely engrossed - تمامًا مغمور أنا (Ana mughmūr tamāman)

- Sound Intonation: A-na mu-GHMOOR ta-MAA-man

39. I'm hooked - معجب أنا (Ana muʿjab)

- Sound Intonation: A-na mu-ʿJAB

40. This is truly fascinating - حقًا مذهل هذا (Haḏā mudh-hil ḥaqan)

- Sound Intonation: ha-DA mudh-HIL ḥa-QAN

Exchanging Contact Information

1. Phone Number - ال هات ف رق م (Raqm al-hātif)

Sound Intonation: ra-QM al-haa-TIF

2. Email Address - ال بري د ع نوان الإل ك تروني (ʿunwān al-barīd al-ʾiliktrūnī)

Sound Intonation: ʿuN-WAA-n al-ba-REED al-i-lik-troo-NEE

3. Contact Information - الات صال مع لومات (Maʿlūmāt al-ittiṣāl)

Sound Intonation: ma-a-loo-MAAT al-i-ti-SAAL

4. Business Card - عمل بِ طاقة (Biṭāqah ʿamal)

Sound Intonation: bi-TAA-qah ʿa-MAL

5. Cell Phone - جوال هاتِ ف (Hātif jawāl)

Sound Intonation: haa-TIF ja-WAAL

6. Social Media - الِ تواصل وسائِ ل الاجِ تماعي (Wasāʾil at-tawāṣul al-ijtimāʿī)

Sound Intonation: wa-saa-IL at-ta-waa-SOOL al-ij-ti-MAA-ee

7. Website - الِ كِ تروني موقِ ع (Mawqīʿ al-kitrūnī)

Sound Intonation: maw-KAA al-ki-troo-NEE

8. LinkedIn Profile - مِ لف LinkedIn (Milf LinkedIn)

Sound Intonation: mil-F LINKED-in

9. Facebook Profile - ملف Facebook (Milf Facebook)

Sound Intonation: mil-F FACE-book

10. Twitter Handle - حساب Twitter (Ḥisāb Twitter)

- Sound Intonation: ḥi-SAAB TWIT-ter

11. Instagram Username - اسم المستخدم على Instagram (Ism al-mustakhdim ʿalā Instagram)

- Sound Intonation: ism al-mus-takh-DIM ʿa-LAA IN-sta-GRAM

12. WhatsApp Number - رقم WhatsApp (Raqm WhatsApp)

- Sound Intonation: ra-QM WHATS-app

13. Skype ID - معرف Skype (Maʿrif Skype)

- Sound Intonation: ma-RIFF SKYPE

14. Zoom Meeting Link - رابط اجتماع Zoom (Rābiṭ ijtimāʿ Zoom)

- Sound Intonation: ra-BEET ij-ti-MAA ZOOM

15. QR Code - رمز الاستجابة السريعة (Rimz al-istijābah as-sarīqah)

- Sound Intonation: rimz al-is-ti-JAA-bah as-sa-REE-qah

16. Let's exchange contact information - لنتبادل معلومات الاتصال (Lanatabādal maʿlūmāt al-ittiṣāl)

- Sound Intonation: la-na-TA-bal ma-a-loo-MAAT al-i-ti-SAAL

17. Can I have your number/email? - هل يمكنني الحصول على رقمك/بريدك الإلكتروني؟ (Hal yumkinuni al-ḥuṣūl ʿalā raqmik/barīdik al-ʾiliktrūnī?)

- Sound Intonation: HAL yu-MKI-nu-ni al-ḥu-SOOL ʿa-LAA raq-MIK/ba-REED-ik al-i-lik-troo-NEE?

18. I'll send you a friend request - سأرسل لك طلب صداقة (Sa'rsilu lak ṭalab ṣadaqah)

- Sound Intonation: sa-AR-si-LU lak ṭa-LAB ṣa-DA-qah

19. Here's my contact info - إليك معلومات الاتصال الخاصة بي (Ilyk maʿlūmāt al-ittiṣāl al-khāṣah bī)

- Sound Intonation: il-YAK ma-a-loo-MAAT al-i-ti-SAAL al-kha-SAH BEE

20. Let's connect on social media - لنتصل على وسائل التواصل الاجتماعي (Lanatṣal ʿalā wasāʾil at-tawāṣul al-ijtimāʿī)

- Sound Intonation: la-na-TSAL ʿa-LAA wa-SAA-il at-ta-WAA-SOOL al-ij-ti-MAA-ee

21. Can you give me your contact details? - هل يمكنك أن تعطيني تفاصيل الاتصال؟ (Hal yumkinuka an taʿṭīnī tafāṣīl al-ittiṣāl?)

- Sound Intonation: HAL yu-MKI-nu-ka an ta-a-ṭEE-nee ta-faa-ṣeel al-i-ti-SAAL?

22. Let's stay in touch - لنبقى على اتصال (Lanabqa ʿalā ittiṣāl)

- Sound Intonation: la-NAB-ka ʿa-LAA it-ti-SAAL

23. I'll message you - ر سالة لك سأرسل (Sa'rsilu lak risālah)

- Sound Intonation: sa-AR-si-LU lak ri-SA-lah

24. Do you use [Social Media Platform]? - ال تواصل و سائل م نصة] ت سـ تخدم هل ؟]الاج تماعي (Hal tastakhdim [manshat wasāʾil at-tawāṣul al-ijtimāʿī]?)

- Sound Intonation: HAL tas-takh-DIM [MAN-shat wa-SAA-il at-ta-waa-SOOL al-ij-ti-MAA-ee]?

25. Let's follow each other - ل ن تابع ال بعض ب عضنا (Lanattābaʿ baʿḍanā al-baʿḍ)

- Sound Intonation: la-na-TAA-ba ba-a-DA-na al-ba-A-d

26. What's your username? - ما اسم المستخدم الخاص بك؟ (Mā ismu al-mustakhdim al-khāṣ bika?)

- Sound Intonation: MAH is-MU al-mus-TAKH-dim al-KHAAS BI-ka?

27. Let me save your number - دعني أحفظ رقمك (Daʿnī ʾaḥfiẓ raqmik)

- Sound Intonation: da-ʿ-NEE aḥ-FIẓ raq-MIK

28. I'll add you as a friend - سأضيفك كصديق (Sa'ḍīfuk kaṣ-ṣadīq)

- Sound Intonation: sa-ḍee-FUK ka-ṣa-ḍeeq

29. Can you send me a request? - هل يمكنك إرسال طلب لي؟ (Hal yumkinuka ʾirsāl ṭalab lī?)

- Sound Intonation: HAL yu-MKI-nu-ka ir-SAAL ṭa-LAB LEE?

30. I'll reach out to you - سأتواصل معك (Sa'tawāṣalu mā'ak)

- Sound Intonation: sa-ta-WAA-sal ma-AK

31. Here's my LinkedIn profile - إليك ملفي في LinkedIn (Ilyk milfī fī LinkedIn)

- Sound Intonation: il-YAK mil-FEE fee LINKED-in

32. I'll send you an invitation - سأرسل لك دعوة (Sa'rsilu lak da'wah)

- Sound Intonation: sa-AR-si-LU lak da-OO-wah

33. Do you have a Viber/Telegram account? - هل لديك حساب Viber/Telegram؟ (Hal ladayka ḥisāb Viber/Telegram?)

- Sound Intonation: HAL la-DAY-ka ḥi-SAAB Viber/Telegram?

34. Let's chat online sometime - لنتحدث عبر الإنترنت في وقت ما (Lantuḥaddath ʿabr al-intarnit fī waqt ma)

- Sound Intonation: lan-tu-ḥad-DA-th ʿa-BR al-in-TAR-net fee WAQT ma

35. Can you add me to your group? - هل يمكنك إضافتي إلى مجموعتك؟ (Hal yumkinuka iḍāfati ilā mujamūʿatik?)

- Sound Intonation: HAL yu-MKI-nu-ka i-ḍaa-FA-tee ilaa mu-ja-MOO-a-tik?

36. Let's share updates - لـ نـ تـ بادل الـ تحديـ ثات (Lanatabādal at-taḥdīṯāt)

- Sound Intonation: la-na-TAA-bal at-ta-ḥDI-thaat

37. What's your preferred messaging app? - لـديك؟ الـ مـ فـضل الـ مـراسـلة تـ طـ بـيق هـو ما (Mā huwa taṭbīq al-murāsalah al-mufaḍḍal ladayk?)

- Sound Intonation: MAH HU-wa tat-BEEK al-mu-raa-SA-la al-mu-FAD-dal la-DAYK?

These phrases will help you smoothly exchange contact information and connect with others in Arabic-speaking contexts. Practice the sound intonations for effective communication.

Numbers and Time

1. Time - وق ت (waqt)

Sound Intonation: waqt

2. Clock - ساعة (sa'ah)

Sound Intonation: sa-AAH

3. Watch - ساعة ي د (sa'ah yad)

Sound Intonation: sa-AAH yad

4. Hour - ساعة (sa'ah)

Sound Intonation: sa-AAH

5. Minute - دق يقة (daqiqah)

Sound Intonation: da-QEE-qah

6. Second - ث ان ية (thaniyah)

Sound Intonation: tha-NEE-yah

7. Day - يـ وم (yawm)

Sound Intonation: yawm

8. Week - أ سـ بوع (usbua')

Sound Intonation: us-BOO-a

9. Month - شـهر (shahr)

Sound Intonation: shar

10. Year - سـنة (sanah)

- Sound Intonation: sa-NAH

11. Today - الـ يوم (alyawm)

- Sound Intonation: al-YAWM

12. Yesterday - أمس (ams)

- Sound Intonation: ams

13. Tomorrow - غدًا (ghadan)

- Sound Intonation: gha-DAN

14. Morning - صـ باح (ṣabah)

- Sound Intonation: ṣa-BAH

15. Evening - مـ ساء (masa')

- Sound Intonation: ma-SA

16. Night - لـ يل (layl)

- Sound Intonation: LAYL

17. Dawn - فـ جر (fajr)

- Sound Intonation: FAJR

18. Dusk - غـ سق (ghasq)

- Sound Intonation: GHASQ

19. Midnight - الـ ليل مـ نـ تـصف (muntaṣaf al-layl)

- Sound Intonation: munt-ASAF al-LAYL

20. Noon - الـ ظهر (adh-duhr)

- Sound Intonation: adh-THOOR

Telling Time

What time is it? - الـ ساعة؟ كم (kam as-sāʿah?)

Sound Intonation: kam as-SA-AH?

It's [number] o'clock - الـ ساعة [number] (as-sāʿah [number])

Sound Intonation: al-SA-AH [number]

It's half past [number] - الـ ساعة الـ آن نـ صف [number] (as-sāʿah al-ān nuṣf [number])

Sound Intonation: al-SA-AH al-AAN nuṣf [number]

It's quarter past [number] - الآ ن ال ساعة ربـ ع [number] (as-sāʿah al-ān rubʿ [number])

Sound Intonation: al-SA-AH al-AAN rubʿ [number]

It's quarter to [number] - إلا الآ ن ال ساعة ربـ ع [number] (as-sāʿah al-ān illā rubʿ [number])

Sound Intonation: al-SA-AH al-AAN illā rubʿ [number]

AM - صباحًا (ṣabāḥan)

Sound Intonation: ṣa-BA-HAN

PM - مساءً (masāʾan)

Sound Intonation: ma-SAA-an

Midnight - ال ل يل م ن ت صف (muntaṣaf al-layl)

Sound Intonation: mun-TA-saf al-LAYL

The time is [number] [AM/PM] - ال وقت الآ ن [number] [AM/PM] (al-waqt al-ān [number] [AM/PM])

Sound Intonation: al-WAQT al-AAN [number] [AM/PM]

Numbers

1. One - واحد (wāḥid)

Sound Intonation: WA-heed

2. Two - اث نان (ithnān)

Sound Intonation: ith-NAHN

3. Three - ث لاث ة (thalāthah)

Sound Intonation: tha-LAA-thah

4. Four - أرب عة (arbaʿah)

Sound Intonation: ar-BAH-a

5. Five - خمسة (khamsah)

Sound Intonation: khams-AH

6. Six - س تة (sittah)

Sound Intonation: sit-TAH

7. Seven - س بعة (sabʿah)

Sound Intonation: sab-AH

8. Eight - ث ماذ ية (thamāniyah)

Sound Intonation: tha-MAH-nee-yah

9. Nine - ت سعة (tisʿah)

Sound Intonation: tis-AH

10. Ten - ع شرة ('asharah)

- Sound Intonation: 'ash-AH-rah

11. Eleven - عشر حدأ (aḥad 'ashar)

- Sound Intonation: a-HAD 'ash-AR

12. Twelve - عشر اث نا (ithnā 'ashar)

- Sound Intonation: ith-NAH 'ash-AR

13. Thirteen - عشر ث لاث ة (thalāthah 'ashar)

- Sound Intonation: tha-LAA-thah 'ash-AR

14. Fourteen - عشر أرب عة (arba'ah 'ashar)

- Sound Intonation: ar-BAH-a 'ash-AR

15. Fifteen - عشر خمسة (khamsah 'ashar)

- Sound Intonation: khams-AH 'ash-AR

16. Sixteen - عشر سـ تة (sittah ʿashar)

- Sound Intonation: sit-TAH ʿash-AR

17. Seventeen - عشر سـ بعة (sabʿah ʿashar)

- Sound Intonation: sab-AH ʿash-AR

18. Eighteen - عشر ثـ مان ية (thamāniyah ʿashar)

- Sound Intonation: tha-MAH-nee-yah ʿash-AR

19. Nineteen - عشر تـ سعة (tisʿah ʿashar)

- Sound Intonation: tis-AH ʿash-AR

20. Twenty - ع شرون (ʿishrūn)

- Sound Intonation: ʿish-ROON

30 - ث لاثون (thalāthūn)

Sound Intonation: tha-LAA-thoon

40 - أرب عون (arbaʿūn)

Sound Intonation: ar-ba-AH-oon

50 - خمسون (khamsūn)

Sound Intonation: khams-OON

60 - س تون (sittūn)

Sound Intonation: sit-TOON

70 - س بعون (sabʿūn)

Sound Intonation: sab-OON

80 - ث مانون (thamānūn)

Sound Intonation: tha-maa-NOON

90 - ت سعون (tisʿūn)

Sound Intonation: tis-OON

100 - مـ ئة (mi'ah)

- Sound Intonation: MEE-ah

1000 - ألـ ف (alf)

- Sound Intonation: alf

One Million - واحد مـ لـ يون (milyūn wāḥid)

- Sound Intonation: mi-lyoon WAH-heed

One Billion - احدو مـ لـ يار (milyār wāḥid)

- Sound Intonation: mi-LYAAR WAH-heed

Days of the Week and Months of the Year

1. **Sunday - الأحد (al-ahad)**

Sound Intonation: al-AH-had

2. Monday - الاث نين (al-ithnayn)

Sound Intonation: al-ith-NAYN

3. Tuesday - ال ثلاث اء (al-thulatha')

Sound Intonation: al-thu-LAA-tha

4. Wednesday - الأرب عاء (al-arba'a)

Sound Intonation: al-ar-BA-a

5. Thursday - ال خم يس (al-khamees)

Sound Intonation: al-kha-MEES

6. Friday - الجمعة (al-jumu'ah)

Sound Intonation: al-ju-MOO-ah

7. Saturday - السبت (al-sabt)

Sound Intonation: al-SABT

These words and phrases will help you when dealing with numbers and telling time in Arabic-speaking contexts.

Months of the Year

1. January - يناير (yanāyir)

Sound Intonation: ya-NA-ir

2. February - فبراير (febrāyir)

Sound Intonation: feb-RA-ir

3. March - مارس (māris)

Sound Intonation: MA-ris

4. April - إبـ ريـ ل (ibrīl)

Sound Intonation: i-BREEL

5. May - مايـ و (māyū)

Sound Intonation: ma-AI-yoo

6. June - يـ وذ يو (yūnīw)

Sound Intonation: yoo-NEE-oo

7. July - يـ ول يو (yūlyū)

Sound Intonation: yoo-LEE-oo

8. August - أغ سطس (aghastis)

Sound Intonation: a-GHAS-tis

9. September - سـ بـ تمـ بر (sebtembir)

Sound Intonation: seb-TEM-bir

10. October - أكتوب ر (oktūbir)

- Sound Intonation: ok-TOO-beer

11. November - نوف م بر (nūfambar)

- Sound Intonation: noo-FAM-bar

12. December - دي سم بر (dīsambir)

- Sound Intonation: dee-SAM-beer

Currencies

Here are some common currencies in Arabic, along with their English translations and sound intonations:

1. Dollar - دولا ر (dūlār)

Sound Intonation: DOO-lar

2. Euro - يـ ورو (yūrū)

Sound Intonation: yoo-ROO

3. Pound - جـ نـ يـه (junayh)

Sound Intonation: joo-NAYH

4. Yen - يـ ن (yen)

Sound Intonation: yen

5. Rupee - روبـ ـية (rubīyah)

Sound Intonation: roo-BEE-yah

6. Rial - ريال (riyāl)

Sound Intonation: ree-YAHL

7. Dinar - دي نار (dīnār)

Sound Intonation: dee-NAHR

8. Franc - ف رنك (farnik)

Sound Intonation: FAR-nik

9. Peso - ب يز و (bīzū)

Sound Intonation: BEE-zoo

10. Won - وون (wūn)

- Sound Intonation: woon

11. Yuan - ي وان (yuān)

- Sound Intonation: yoo-AHN

12. Lira - ل يرة (līrah)

- Sound Intonation: LEE-rah

13. Krona - كرون ا (krunā)

- Sound Intonation: kroo-NAH

14. Shekel - ش يقل (sheqel)

- Sound Intonation: SHE-kel

15. Ringgit - رن جت (ringgit)

- Sound Intonation: RING-git

16. Baht - ب ات (baht)

- Sound Intonation: baht

17. Zloty - زل وتي (zloty)

- Sound Intonation: ZLO-tee

18. Dirham - درهم (dirham)

- Sound Intonation: DEER-ham

19. Riyal - ريال (riyal)

- Sound Intonation: ree-YAH

Conclusion

In conclusion, the "Everyday Arabic Phrasebook for Dubai Travelers" is an invaluable companion for anyone planning to visit Dubai or any Arabic-speaking region.

It provides a comprehensive collection of essential phrases and expressions, making it easier for travelers to navigate daily interactions, communicate their needs, and immerse themselves in the local culture.

From greetings and polite expressions to practical phrases for getting around, ordering food, shopping, and seeking medical assistance, this phrasebook covers a wide range of situations travelers may encounter.

The inclusion of sound intonations ensures that users can pronounce Arabic phrases accurately, enhancing their ability to connect with locals and create meaningful experiences during their journey.

Whether you're a seasoned traveler or embarking on your first adventure to Dubai, this phrasebook equips you with the language tools you need to communicate effectively and confidently.

By embracing the local language, you'll not only enhance your travel experience but also show respect for the culture and people you encounter along the way.

We hope that this phrasebook serves as a valuable resource and enhances your travel experience in Dubai, allowing you to connect with locals, explore the city's rich heritage, and create lasting memories during your stay. Safe travels!

Printed in Great Britain
by Amazon

40104755R00109